WRESTLING WITH DISCIPLESHIP

CHAD O. DAVIDSON

GoodFight

CONTENTS

Introduction — ix

Chapter 1 — 1
The Bible says Imitate God...Therefore, I Wrestle

Chapter 2 — 8
What is Discipleship?

Chapter 3 — 19
How God Pinned Me Down!

Chapter 4 — 37
Discipleship in the Early Church

Chapter 5 — 46
Discipleship Through God's Word

Chapter 6 — 59
Discipleship Through the Fear of the Lord

Chapter 7 — 75
Proper Foundation: Are You in Your Stance?

Chapter 8 — 83
Discipleship Through Witnessing?

Chapter 9 — 96
Knowing Your Enemy in the Context of Discipleship

Chapter 10 — 104
The Toughest Battle for a Disciple

Chapter 11 — 114
Finishing the Race Set Before Us By Joe Schimmel

Chapter 12 — 132
Discipling Through the Seven Churches of Revelation

Chapter 13 — 139
Embrace the Grind

Chapter 14 — 149
Our Last Match

Notes	157
Acknowledgments	161
About the Author	163

Copyright © 2024 by Fight the Good Fight Ministries Inc.
All rights reserved. Library of Congress Control Number: 2024930085

No part of this publication may be reproduced, stored, or transmitted in any form or by any means: electronic, mechanical, digital, photocopy, recording, or any other, except for brief quotations in printed reviews without permission from the publisher. For permission, contact Good Fight Publishing. www.goodfight.org.

Edits & Proofreading: Ted Hollis, Melissa Service, and Tony Palacio
Interior Design: Melissa Service
Book Cover Design: Tony Palacio
Cover Image: freechristimages.com: used with permission
Production Managers: Doug Stebleton & Tony Palacio
Keith Green: Asleep in the Light: Copyright@1979 Ears to Hear Music (ASCAP) (Admin: CapitolCMGPublishing.com) All Rights reserved. Used with Permission.

First Edition 2024
ISBN: 979-8-9885940-3-1 Paperback
ISBN: 979-8-9885940-4-8 E-book

Scripture quotations taken from the (NASB®) New American Standard Bible®, Copyright © 1960, 1971, 1977, 1995 by The Lockman Foundation. Used by permission. All rights reserved. www.Lockman.org.

This book is dedicated to my beautiful wife, Holly Davidson, as well as my children, Eli, Justus, Ariella, and Galilee. It is also dedicated to all the wrestlers I've been blessed enough to coach over the years, and to the men who have discipled me.

INTRODUCTION

In an interview that Mark Munoz gave prior to fighting Chris Leben at UFC 136, a fight which Mark would win by TKO in the second round, the fighter who would come to be known as "The Filipino Wrecking Machine" stated:

"I have the spirit of my Lord and Savior Jesus Christ [...] And I [have] faith that he has put me in this position."[1]

While that position would lead him to a solid career in the UFC, there was a position he held back in 2004 that he probably does not often recall, though it will always remain in my memory. Mark was a late replacement at a wrestling camp in Squaw Valley (now known as Palisades Tahoe), California, to show technique at the Hitchcock/Azevedo Wrestling Camp. I do not believe he was placed there by accident, but by God's own grace and foreknowledge of how he would be used.

His unexpected presence became a divine appointment, and

I absorbed his technical sessions as if they were gospel truths. The significance of this encounter was not in what was actually taught as wrestling technique, but in what he would share after his technique sessions had finished. Coach John Acevedo, a man of faith and the director of the camp, orchestrated a divine plan for the camp's conclusion—a plan where the counselors would transcend the tactical victories of wrestling to share the profound truths of the Gospel. Mark Munoz, one of my wrestling idols, shared his testimony, which ended up being far more important than anything he shared on the wrestling mat.

He told of his journey of faith as a young man from Vallejo, California, and the transformative power of Christ in his life. While that wasn't the moment that I gave my life to Christ, there was someone I looked up to who was willing to share with me what Christ had done in their life, and that garnered my undivided attention. If it was just some random person on the street, I don't know that I would have paid as close attention. However, looking up to someone who is teaching you something already makes you stand at attention when they share with you other truths that they have come to learn.

In short, I listened to Mark because he was already someone I wanted to learn from, and because his testimony was something that came back to my mind later in life—just prior to my conversion.

I want to introduce this book as a reminder of how anyone can use anything they put their minds to in order to share the Gospel with others. In the tapestry of life, our journey with Christ is a narrative woven with victories and defeats, a relentless wrestling match that transcends time and space. The epic battle that unfolded on Calvary's hill, waged by Jesus, resonates this victory with our own struggles, transforming our fight into a celebration of a battle already won. Yet this doesn't diminish the significance of our own personal wrestling matches. On the contrary, it underscores the eternal impact of our struggles, not only for ourselves, but for the lives we touch during our earthly sojourn.

This book, *Wrestling With Discipleship*, stands as a testament to the profound truth that anything we dedicate our minds to becomes a vessel for spreading the Gospel. Whether it's wrestling or cheerleading, housework or handiwork, using whatever our hands are doing in the moment to bring forth the truth of the Gospel will have a radical impact on someone we might never consider. My testimony is shared in chapter 2, and this seed is one that helped find fertile ground because of the work that was previously done.

How can you use whatever you are capable of to help further the cause of Christ? How can you use your experience in life to help bring forth the truth of Scripture and lead people to the One who died and rose again for them?

CHAPTER 1

THE BIBLE SAYS IMITATE GOD... THEREFORE, I WRESTLE

"If the wrestler is unable to overcome Jacob spiritually, it is because Jacob is not willing to yield."
– John H. Walton

As an assistant coach at my alma mater, one thing I was blessed enough to do every year was an optional practice where I would take the team on a hike up a hill to a cross on Mount McCoy in Simi Valley, California. The cross on the west end of town was so high you could look out and see every inch of our city. It was there that I would share my testimony, have an opportunity to share the Gospel, and pray over our team during the Christmas break.

I used to give a similar message, but it always had to do with one story I found in the Bible concerning wrestling. On the night I came to Christ, I remember going to my computer to try and find wrestling in the Bible. To my surprise, Scripture not only discussed wrestling, but it was *who* was doing the wrestling that really surprised me.

> *"Then Jacob was left alone, and a man wrestled with him until daybreak. When he saw that he had not prevailed against him, he touched the socket of his thigh; so, the socket of Jacob's thigh was dislocated while he wrestled with him. Then he said, 'Let me go, for the dawn is breaking.' But he said, 'I will not let you go unless you bless me.' So, he said to him, 'What is your name?' And he said, 'Jacob.' He said, 'Your name shall no longer be Jacob, but Israel; for you have striven with God and with men and have prevailed.' Then Jacob asked him and said, 'Please tell me your name.' But he said, 'Why is it that you ask my name?' And he blessed him there. So, Jacob named the place Penuel, for he said, 'I have seen God face to face, yet my life has been preserved.' Now the sun rose upon him just as he crossed over Penuel, and he was limping on his thigh. Therefore, to this day the sons of Israel do not eat the sinew of the hip, which is on the socket of the thigh, because he touched the socket of Jacob's thigh in the sinew of the hip"* (Genesis 32:24-32).

What sticks out most regarding this encounter is not that Jacob was taken down by a hip toss but that he realized that it was God Himself with whom he was wrestling. "I have seen God face to face, yet my life has been preserved."

Jacob knew that such an encounter, apart from the grace of God, would typically end with the loss of one's life. But he was blessed enough not only to see God and live, but to wrestle Him and not die. From this text we can conclude that… God is a wrestler!

The Apostle Paul encouraged the church in Ephesus to "Be imitators of God, therefore, as beloved children" (Ephesians 5:1). Therefore, when we see that God is a wrestler, we need to ensure we are wrestling. So, what kind of wrestling should we be doing?

Ephesians 6:12 explains: "It is not with flesh and blood, but against the rulers, against the powers, against the world forces of this darkness, against the spiritual forces of wickedness in the heavenly places."

This wrestling is not uncommon to man, but is one in which many of us will engage. We may not get the chance to wrestle with a physical manifestation of God like Jacob, but each of us have had our own instances of wrestling with the God of the universe, spiritually. We have all fallen into sin and have need of a Savior. The great patriarch of the faith, Jacob, was no different in this regard. While his wrestling match with God was physical and provided a spiritual change that would echo for eternity, Jacob had been wrestling with God long before their encounter in Penuel. In fact, Jacob was a known deceiver. Jacob even deceived his own brother, who was the superior hunter-gatherer, to give him his entire birthright for a cup of soup.

"When the boys grew up, Esau became a skillful hunter, a man of the field, but Jacob was a peaceful man, living in tents. Now

Isaac loved Esau, because he had a taste for game, but Rebekah loved Jacob. When Jacob had cooked stew, Esau came in from the field and he was famished; and Esau said to Jacob, 'Please let me have a swallow of that red stuff there, for I am famished.' Therefore, his name was called Edom. But Jacob said, 'First sell me your birthright.' Esau said, 'Behold, I am about to die; so of what use then is the birthright to me?' And Jacob said, 'First swear to me'; so, he swore to him, and sold his birthright to Jacob. Then Jacob gave Esau bread and lentil stew; and he ate and drank and rose and went on his way. Thus, Esau despised his birthright" (Genesis 25:27-34).

This would not be the only time Jacob used his mischievous nature in order to get what he wanted from his brother Esau. He even took his mom's advice in order to receive the blessing from his father Isaac.

In Genesis chapter 27, we read that Rebekah came up with a plot to deceive Isaac into giving Jacob, instead of Esau, the blessing reserved for the firstborn son. Rebekah advises Jacob to impersonate Esau by wearing his brother's clothes and using goat skins to imitate Esau's hairiness. Jacob complies and prepares a meal for his father Isaac. Approaching blind Isaac, Jacob pretends to be Esau and, despite his doubts, Isaac blesses Jacob with prosperity, authority, and divine favor.

"And he said, 'Are you really my son Esau?' And he said, 'I am.' So, he said, 'Bring it to me, and I will eat of my son's game, that I may bless you.' And he brought it to him, and he ate; he also

brought him wine and he drank. Then his father Isaac said to him, 'Please come close and kiss me, my son.' So he came close and kissed him; and when he smelled the smell of his garments, he blessed him and said, 'See, the smell of my son is like the smell of a field which the LORD has blessed; Now may God give you of the dew of heaven, And of the fatness of the earth, and an abundance of grain and new wine; may peoples serve you, and nations bow down to you; be master of your brothers, and may your mother's sons bow down to you. Cursed be those who curse you, and blessed be those who bless you'" (Genesis 27:24-29).

However, almost immediately after receiving the blessing, his brother Esau and father Isaac knew what he had done.

"Now it came about, as soon as Isaac had finished blessing Jacob, and Jacob had hardly gone out from the presence of Isaac his father, that Esau his brother came in from his hunting. Then he also made savory food and brought it to his father; and he said to his father, 'Let my father arise and eat of his son's game, that you may bless me.' Isaac his father said to him, 'Who are you?' And he said, 'I am your son, your firstborn, Esau.' Then Isaac trembled violently, and said, 'Who was he then that hunted game and brought it to me, so that I ate of all of it before you came, and blessed him? Yes, and he shall be blessed.' When Esau heard the words of his father, he cried out with an exceedingly great and bitter cry, and said to his father, 'Bless me, even me also, O my father!' And he said, 'Your

brother came deceitfully and has taken away your blessing'" (Genesis 27:30-35).

This exchange made Esau's heart turn against Jacob and created a root of bitterness that only subsided, apparently for a short time, after Jacob came into his own personal relationship with God. Prior to his wrestling match with God, Jacob only referred to God as the God of his forefathers.

In verse 9 of the same chapter in which he wrestled with God, you can actually see Jacob refer to God as: "O God of my father Abraham and God of my father Isaac, O LORD." Notice how He is referring to God as the God of his Father. Jacob's life of mischief and deceit apparently kept him from having intimacy with God that his father and grandfather had with Yahweh. It wasn't until he was brought face-to-face with God in that wrestling match, and shown grace by his brother Esau, that Jacob (now named Israel) recognized God not only as the God of his forefathers, but also the God who was personal to him. In Genesis chapter 33 verse 20, we read, *"Then, he erected there an altar and called it El elohe Israel."*

El elohe Israel means "God, the God of Israel." No longer was this relationship merely the hereditary nature of his father's relationship, but as he began to live a life free of deceit, he began to know his God more intimately. I pray this can be a lesson for all of us, as we have all had our own wrestling matches with God. Maybe you think of God as an excellent answer for your philosophical questions. Maybe God has been a hereditary piece of your American dream that has been passed down to you by your family. Maybe your version of God resembles a genie to whom you think you can bother with requests when you are in trouble or in need of something. Let Jacob's story be a lesson to you to make sure God is your personal God and not simply the God of your friends or family. Make your relationship with Him personal and live in peace, regardless of circumstance.

This is a time in which you need to tap out, as we say in wrestling. If you are wrestling with God, recognize your own futility and His great goodness. The Apostle Paul came to realize this through his own trials when he wrote, "...for Christ's sake; for when I am weak, then I am strong" (2 Corinthians 12:10).

When you come to Christ, not only will you realize we do all things through His strength, but that He is on our team – and we are on His! When you face trials and temptations, He is there (1 Corinthians 10:13). When you feel weak and weighed down, He brings rest (Matthew 11:28). If you aren't for Him, you are against Him (Matthew 12:30).

So, if you are still wrestling against Him, get off the losing team and leave the dominion of darkness for the Kingdom of His Beloved Son (Colossians 1:13), and become more than a conqueror through Him who loves us (Romans 8:37)!

CHAPTER 2
WHAT IS DISCIPLESHIP?

"In the New Testament, salvation and discipleship are so closely related as to be indivisible."
– A.W. Tozer

When my wife and I first began our relationship, she was a nanny for a couple at our church. I was twenty-two years old and had started my coaching career as an assistant coach at my alma mater. I still remember the first time my wife and I went to her place of work and a few of the questions her boss asked me. Sitting next to my pastor and future father-in-law, he asked me if I thought I could take Pastor Joe in a fight. It was quite an interesting question to be asked, but the modus operandi of my wife's boss, Bob, was to make people uncomfortable.

My wife was more than just someone who worked for his

family; she was the daughter of one of his closest friends. I sidestepped the question and told him I wasn't sure.

He replied, "Would you be able to take me," to which I said, "Absolutely."

Now, for most people hearing that, you probably wonder what on earth would make someone ask me that? Well, at that time I was training in MMA, and Bob knew I was a wrestler. He was checking my confidence level, but he also knew I was someone who loved to train in martial arts. Bob also knew that if I was the person I was claiming to be, I wouldn't be offended by a bit of fun.

On the other hand, Bob's wife was very nice to me and never asked me if I could take her or my future mother-in-law in a fight—not that she would have anyway. But she also had a much different idea in her head regarding the fact that I was a wrestler. You see, my future wife told her I was a wrestler, and when my wife conveyed that fact, she assumed that Marti, Bob's wife, understood what my wife meant when she said I was coaching wrestlers. But what Marti actually had in mind was me in tights, jumping off turnbuckles, waiting for a ref to slap the mat three times, and announcing the winner of the Intercontinental WWE Championship. I'm sure her view of me was far different from what her husband perceived when I visited their house!

It's essential to realize that having the correct vocabulary with a wrong definition or an unclear understanding can lead to very different, incorrect conclusions. If you believe that "discipleship" is a secondary Christian position that takes place after you become a more mature Christian, you will believe something contrary to what God's Word describes as the proper definition of what it means to be a disciple.

So... what is the true meaning of discipleship?

The title of this book, *Wrestling with Discipleship*, is a play on words. It presents my own wrestling stories reflecting the truth that most people *wrestle* with this topic. If you watched ten sermons on discipleship, you would probably hear five to ten different definitions and ten ways to accomplish it. This chapter presents what the Bible teaches on discipleship and how we can begin to live out the discipleship of the apostles and our Lord Jesus Christ!

You may be surprised to learn that the English word "discipleship" never occurs in the New Testament. Does this mean that discipleship isn't found in the Bible? Absolutely not. What it means is we have a word used to describe an idea we find in the writings of the biblical text.

Theology is the study of the nature of God and religious belief. If someone says we don't see discipleship in the Bible, that wouldn't be the truth, the whole truth, and nothing but the truth. It is true the specific word for discipleship doesn't appear in the biblical texts, but this is where we find the greatest source of truth on the subject. The term simply describes, by way of a word, what we find the apostles doing in the Bible as they follow and learn from Jesus.

Although the noun "discipleship" isn't used in the Bible, there are both verb and noun usages for the term disciple. The two Greek words are "mathetes" (the noun) and "matheteo" (the verb). The former is most commonly used to describe the disciples of Christ, while the latter is used for "soul-winning" or evangelism in the book of Acts. *"After they had preached the gospel to that city and had made many disciples, they returned to Lystra and to Iconium and to Antioch"* (Acts 14:21).

It is also used for the entire process and even the practice of teaching believers what Jesus has taught. An example can be found in Matthew chapter 28, verses 17-20: *"When they saw Him, they worshiped Him; but some were doubtful. And Jesus came up and spoke to them, saying, 'All authority has been given to Me in heaven and on earth. Go therefore and make disciples of all the nations, baptizing them in the name of the Father and the Son and the Holy Spirit, teaching them to observe all that I commanded you; and lo, I am with you always, even to the end of the age.'"*

While these are two ways we find the terminology used in the New Testament, there are additional Old Testament texts which describe the practice without employing modern terminology. *"He who walks with wise men will be wise, But the companion of fools will suffer harm"* (Proverbs 13:20).

Walking with the wise will make you wise. Psalm 1 gives a warning to those who sit with scoffers and do not meditate upon God's Word which is a necessity for all those who love God. But Proverbs doesn't just warn us of being a companion of fools. It also shows us the importance of being humble and accepting correction. *"He whose ear listens to the life-giving reproof will dwell among the wise. He who neglects discipline despises himself, but he who listens to reproof acquires under-*

standing. The fear of the Lord is the instruction for wisdom, and before honor comes humility" (Proverbs 15:31-33).

We are told those who live out a life lacking in biblical discipline will be blown away by the wind. In the New Testament, those who do not follow Jesus' commands will be "tossed to and fro by every wind of doctrine" (Ephesians 4:14).

There are many texts similar to this that we find in the wisdom category of Scripture, but it is important to ascertain what Jesus and the apostles believed about the subject. This is essential because some want to make salvation and discipleship so dissimilar that they present them as two wholly different concepts. However, A.W. Tozer gives us great insight into the differences and similarities between discipleship and salvation. Tozer writes, "They are not identical, but as with Siamese twins, they are joined by a tie which can be severed only at the price of death."[1]

While discipleship is not a precise synonym for salvation, in the New Testament, the terms disciple and "Christian" seem to range from either very close or fully synonymous in their usage. That is to say, a Christian is a disciple in the same way that a disciple is a Christian. In fact, the first time we actually see the term "Christian" used, it was an insulting label that was applied to those following Jesus. "...and the disciples were first called Christians in Antioch" (Acts 11:26b).

A "Christian," like a disciple, could be identified by how they followed the example of their master so closely that those observing their conduct could clearly spot them. This helps us best understand what Peter meant when he used the word

"Hupogrammos" to describe how closely a Christian should follow the example of Christ. *"For you have been called for this purpose, since Christ also suffered for you, leaving you an example for you to follow in His steps"* (1 Peter 2:21).

This example was one that dealt with the conduct of the believer, as Christians are called to be "conformed to the image of His Son [Jesus]" (Romans 8:29). So, this calling requires us to conform to the image of Christ by the way we lead our lives. We see further evidence of this in 1 Peter 2:22-25 where it is written: *"Who committed no sin, nor was any deceit found in his mouth; and while being reviled, he did not revile in return; while suffering, he uttered no threats, but kept entrusting himself to him who judges righteously; and he himself bore our sins in his body on the cross, so that we might die to sin and live to righteousness; for by his wounds you were healed. For you were continually straying like sheep, but now you have returned to the shepherd and guardian of your souls."*

While the theme of becoming more and more like Jesus is frequently referenced throughout the New Testament epistles, the aforementioned "Hupogrammos" speaks to the intimate nature of following in Jesus' footsteps. The word "hupogrammos" is explained this way: "An example (ὑπογραμμὸν). Only here in the New Testament. A graphic word, meaning a copy set by writing-masters for their pupils. Some explain it as a copy of characters over which the student is to trace the lines."[2]

It is upon tracing the "ABCs" of Jesus' life by which we ultimately become a disciple. This emulation brings us to what Jesus said would happen to those who are "fully trained." Luke chapter 6, verse 40 says it like this: *"A pupil is not above his teacher; but everyone, after he has been fully trained, will be like his teacher."*

In the epistle of 1 Peter, we see one of the few usages of the term "Christian" in the manner to which believers are called. *"But if anyone suffers as a Christian, he is not to be ashamed, but is to glorify God in this name"* (1 Peter 4:16).

Not only should the outside world look at us and know we have a hope within us that is far greater than anything offered outside of Christ, but they should also know how we love our Savior by the way we live our lives and the way we show our love. The book of John chapter 13, verse 35 says, *"By this all men will know that you are My disciples, if you have love for one another."*

This was a key factor in Christ's ministry: His own would begin to look and love like Him. The believer is actually predestined to be conformed to the image of His Son (Romans 8:29), and we are to take every thought captive to the obedience of Christ (2 Corinthians 10:5). We are to love as He loved, and we are to walk in the ways of our Master.

If we are going to fully understand the way in which Jesus taught His followers, it is important for us to look at how the Jewish people taught their children before God became a man in the person of Jesus Christ!

In Martina Gracin's paper, *Discipleship in the Context of Judaism in Jesus' Time: Part 1*, she points out that multiple scholars, such as Ikechukwu Michael Oluikpe and Lois Tverberg, speak of the multi-stage teaching of Jewish boys prior to

Jesus' birth in Bethlehem. Gracin writes, "Three stages of education within Judaism of Jesus' time were: *Bet Sefer*, *Bet Talmud*, and *Bet Midrash*. Each stage included specific age-group of Jewish boys."[3]

These stages would be used as guardrails in the Jewish culture against the growing Hellenistic culture in which they were born. Gracin further expands upon Oluikpe's premise that the trifold approach was presented as follows:

> "It is generally assumed that studying of the Mishna starts at *Bet Talmud*, a second stage of Jewish education. Horbury (1999, 85) expresses his doubts in that assumption saying that sources that we have are remarkably vague about the curriculum of the Bet Talmud. These sources basically state this stage of education was devoted to the study of the Oral Torah, which could have meant fuller and deeper commentary of the Bible. The rabbis may have possibly tried to turn the higher levels of elementary education as an introduction and preparation for Bet Midrash, but it is questionable whether serious study of Halakha would start before Bet Midrash (cf. Horbury 1999, 85). The term comes from the verb halach ("to walk") and stand for observation of the Torah. This term is also used for stipulations from the system of Halakhah.
>
> After twelve or thirteen, gifted students joined the *Beth Midrash* ("House of Study") where the focus was understanding and applying the Torah and oral tradition to daily life in a more intense way. Study was conducted under a

famous rabbi. The student, usually called a *talmid* (disciple), would attach himself to and travel with the rabbi as part of his education. His goal was to become like his rabbi and learn his *halakoth* until he internalized it... This continued until he became a full-fledged rabbi or scribe at the age of thirty. Without training at the *Beth Midrash*, a man could not be recognized as formally educated. Though the first two stages (elementary schools) seemed to have been affordable and accessible to the average Jewish boy, the third stage (higher schools/rabbinic academies) seemed to be for boys who were intelligent, talented and from well-to-do homes."[4]

The Jewish people kept a continuous education model in order to prevent their children from becoming like the world around them. The Jewish people knew the Hellenistic ways of mixing Jewish thoughts and beliefs with Greek practices were never going to be what the God of Israel made clear to them, nor was it a part of the commands He laid out. Such a focus on discipling one's mind should be a great objective of ours, as the culture around us continues to attempt to permeate the church and effect decisions and lifestyles of those professing Christ. This hyper-focus on understanding the laws of God and the teachings of those in authority (the idea of being a disciple in the third stage, "talmid") is what we are talking about now.

As Lois Tverberg writes: "A disciple was expected to leave his family and job to join the rabbi in his austere lifestyle. Disciples would live with the rabbi twenty-four hours a day, walking from town to town, teaching, working, eating, and studying.

They would discuss the scriptures and apply them to their lives. The disciples were also supposed to be the rabbi's servants, submitting to his authority while they served his needs. Indeed, the word 'rabbi' means 'my master,' and was a term of great respect."[5]

This would mean the discipling that Jesus practiced and preached would be far different from the typical discipling we are accustomed to in today's church. The idea of discipleship was meant to incorporate brothers into your life, not just simply give them life lessons. A disciple should know your children and be involved in everything you do. In fact, Tverberg points out that there is an ancient Midrash that explains that being disciples involved being so close to someone that you begin collecting their dust! *"Let your home be a meeting place for the wise; dust yourself in the soil of their feet, and drink thirstily of their words."* She observes that the middle line reads, *"dust yourself in the soil of their feet,"* is sometimes translated as *"sit amid the dust of their feet."*

Today, it is next to impossible to even conceive such a practice. But for Jesus and His followers, this was something normative to His culture and needs a resurrection in ours! It makes complete sense that Jesus would have disciples because every Rabbi had a group of students.

The Apostle Paul, prior to his fateful meeting with Christ on the road to Damascus, was discipled by Gamaliel. He taught Paul to become a zealous Jewish teacher, and this zeal is mentioned in Acts chapter 5 when Paul shared his testimony. *"I am a Jew, born in Tarsus of Cilicia, but brought up in this city, educated under Gamaliel, strictly according to the law of our fathers, being zealous for God just as you all are today"* (Acts 22:3).

Like Paul, who was taught by Gamaliel and eventually followed the teachings of Christ, we need to make sure we are getting ourselves dusty from the people who are discipling us. Get involved in sharing the Gospel and get to know those who are discipling you on a personal level. This will allow for true discipleship and a much more biblical way of learning and growing in your walk with Christ.

IN SUMMARY: WHAT IS DISCIPLESHIP?

It is the practice of living and learning from those who know Jesus. Discipleship shows us how to live and follow the will of God for our lives. As we move forward, let's think of discipleship in this manner, and let us be carried forward as we continue to wrestle with being discipled by Christ and His followers!

CHAPTER 3
HOW GOD PINNED ME DOWN!

"You will never cease to be the most amazed person on earth at what God has done for you on the inside."
– Oswald Chambers

IN MY YOUTH, my summers were filled with camping, boating, and visiting family. Winters brought dirt bike riding and getting spoiled on Christmas. I led the league in scoring in basketball (until the realization of my height deficiency), played all-star baseball, and got to play on football teams with guys who would eventually play in the NFL. I was also a gifted student and was even voted in as student council president. Plenty of people have shared their reason for not initially understanding the love of God - because their family did not show it to them. But that wasn't my case at all.

I was loved and blessed by my family and grew up knowing

they cared for me. While living a relatively orderly life as a child, it wasn't until I entered the third grade that my life changed in a big way. My parents chose to adopt my cousins. My aunt was pregnant with my younger sister when the adoption process began. She and her husband were investigated for child abuse and were eventually convicted. They received 18 years in prison—a timeframe that was placed upon them so their children would be adults.

I bonded immediately with my cousin, who became my older brother. We were as close as biological siblings. As cousins, we would play together during holidays or get-togethers, but when he became my brother, I never thought of him as anything else. He was the reason I became a wrestler. I looked up to him because I honestly thought he was the coolest guy I had met near my own age. He and I had lived very different lives and I was pretty ignorant of a lot of life's intricacies at that point. A key example of those differences was stored in the cabinet above the refrigerator.

My dad was a mechanic at UPS and a common gift the drivers would give to their mechanics were bottles of liquor. My dad, prior to fully surrendering to Christ, wasn't much of a liquor drinker. He was more of a beer man, so the alcohol in the cupboard went untouched. That is until my brother showed it to me. In all honesty, I didn't think much of it when we first started taking shots when my parents were out shopping. But that taste of alcohol developed into a habit, and I began to drink at different parties that were thrown on my street, specifically in the areas where they would send the younger people to hang out. By the time I got to middle school, I drank almost every weekend, and by the time I reached high school, I drank nearly every day.

WRESTLING DRUNK

Alcohol would prove to be my ultimate downfall as a wrestler, and it almost cost me my life. In fact, it was during my senior year when it really started to ruin some of the hard work I had done to prepare myself for my final year as a Royal High School wrestler. I played other sports growing up, and achieved a number of substantial goals, but none of them compared to my goal of winning a CIF Championship. As team captain, a win would stamp my ticket to the state tournament. But a night of drinking, which turned into a drunken day, would end the reality of that dream.

It happened a couple of weeks before the league finals tournament. I was out with a friend and had not really thought much about the smaller local tournament I was going to compete in that weekend. After going through a tough tournament cycle, I thought it would be cool to get another win under my belt to help my record look a little better. I had fallen asleep before the match, but my friend woke me up and helped me get to the school before the team bus left. I thought my friend had saved me from getting in trouble, but little did I know what was about to come!

I won the first couple matches without much of an issue. The quarterfinal match was a little tougher, but I was still able to win without much stress. However, the semi-final match was harder than I expected. While wrestling in the bottom position, I did something I learned at one of my first practices not to do. I was lifted in the air, and instead of bracing myself for a standing switch, I put my arms backwards to land (something you should never, ever do), no doubt because of my still-drunken state. By the time I reversed him, I looked over and saw that my thumb was not in the correct position. I attempted to put it back in place, but couldn't, and I had to forfeit the match. I went to the doctor's office the next day and received a note which said I wouldn't be able to hold a pencil for a few months. Trying to get out of doing my classwork, I gave to my teachers, but I never gave my coach that note. I wrestled the rest of the season, taping my hand up the best I could, finishing a few weeks later. Because of my drunken night - and delayed and silly reactions - I did not accomplish the goals I had set out for myself. I wrestled all of the post-season without being able to practice, and even though we achieved the team goal of becoming two-time CIF Champions, my individual goal of qualifying for State did not happen.

    This should have awakened me to what drinking was doing to my life, but it wasn't the wake-up call it should have been. This loss of the recognition I so badly wanted did nothing to curb my appetite for alcohol but instead only hardened my heart even more. The next big event in my life, which would be far worse than not realizing my potential as a wrestler, was one that almost led me to my ultimate end.

HIT-AND-RUN/DUI

With my friend playing the role of the designated driver, I went to the local carnival and drank myself into a drunken stupor. When I got home, I sent some texts to a few people to see if they were still up. A couple of them replied, so, I got behind the wheel of my Suburban while being completely inebriated. I was so drunk that I went the wrong way and put my car on cruise control in a residential neighborhood before passing out. When I came to, I ripped through a mailbox and tree that landed on someone's house. The people living in the house ran out and chased me down, but I sped off and went to hang out at my friend's house. A tree branch was sticking out of my radiator when I got there.

After a while, I headed home, and as I drove down the street and crested the hill, my car stalled. Someone who knew me attempted to help me park my broken-down car, and while trying to do this, I fell. I was not in my right mind, and because of this, the car rolled over my arm before hitting a pickup truck. As I was getting back in my car, the truck owner's daughter began yelling. I tried to start my car. I didn't believe it would actually turn over, but I wanted to roll up the window so I could drown out the woman's yelling! But much to my surprise, the car started, and I immediately drove away, racing toward home.

The young man who had stopped to help me told the truck owner he would follow me to get my license plate number. He tracked my tumultuous route home—making sure I arrived safely, then returned to let the owners know he couldn't get the plate. Much to his surprise, they didn't need it. My wallet had fallen out at the scene, and I was destined for a DUI and the hit-and-run that I deserved.

I remember telling this story at my court-ordered AA meetings, and everyone told me how unlucky I was my wallet fell out of the car. While that would make sense for those hearing the story without an eternal perspective, the truth was... God used that wallet to save my life! I'm convinced Satan helped my car to start. I think he put people there to try to get me out of trouble, but I believe God made sure I got caught. Although, at the time, getting apprehended caused me to harden my heart toward God, it was the starting point for me to be broken down enough so that my heart would be in a proper place to receive the Gospel.

When things stop going your way, and you begin to blame others, it becomes difficult to look at yourself and see that *you* are the problem. Just as Eve in the garden blamed the serpent (Satan) when she ate from the Tree of the Knowledge of Good and Evil, and Adam blamed Eve (and even went as far as blaming God for making her), it seems to be in man's fallen nature to blame someone else for their own sin.

This was definitely the case for me when I ultimately became an atheist in church. You see, a friend had invited me to go to church with him, and I really didn't think much of it. I was still relatively conservative and would have thought of myself as a Christian, even if all of the evidence pointed to the contrary. The night before church, I had a party at my house, and as usual, there would be a number of people who would exclusively hang out in my room. To my surprise, the same people who had made their sinful abode in my room were the same ones I saw at church in that morning.

I was there looking for a reason to have hope in my life, but all I saw were people sitting or standing in the pews with their arms raised in worship. I saw the hypocrisy of lip-service religion and abandoned any belief that there was a God. While I don't know where their hearts were concerning the Lord, from my vantage point, their hypocrisy in plain sight was altogether what I needed to deny the existence of God.

I did this by denying the "god" that I had believed in for most of my life—which was a "god" I had formed in my own image. The god I had served for so much of my life was a god that only existed as a figment of my own imagination. I was breaking the first two commandments given on Mount Sinai. I was worshiping a god whom I had formed into being whatever I wanted him to be. Ultimately, I was upset that this god was no longer serving my needs, and I ignorantly rejected the true God in his stead. Truth be told, atheism is merely a form of idolatry, and that's what I was engaging in. The book of Romans puts it this way:

> *"For the wrath of God is revealed from heaven against all ungodliness and unrighteousness of men who suppress the truth in unrighteousness, because that which is known about God is evident within them; for God made it evident to them. For since the creation of the world His invisible attributes, His eternal*

power and divine nature, have been clearly seen, being understood through what has been made, so that they are without excuse. For even though they knew God, they did not honor Him as God or give thanks, but they became futile in their speculations, and their foolish hearts were darkened. Professing to be wise, they became fools, and exchanged the glory of the incorruptible God for an image in the form of corruptible man and of birds and four-footed animals and crawling creatures" (Romans 1:18-23).

I began to suppress this truth—to the point I even hated the God in whom I claimed I didn't believe in. I became the kid turning the Jack-in-the-Box crank while holding down the lid and claiming that God wouldn't pop out because He wasn't real. But the truth was that my foolish heart was being darkened by my sin, and I was suppressing the truth. Sin had become the norm for me, and it had led me into a dark and depressed state. I had no hope in the world, and so I was living hopelessly.

WRESTLING TEAMMATE BEGINS REACHING OUT

I was on a path of destruction, and anyone around me was going to be affected by my choices. I was playing into the devil's hands, and I was so destructive that some of my friends decided they needed to distance themselves from me. Some of them chose this path because of practical wisdom, but others were finding the truth in Jesus Christ.

My friend and former team captain, Adam, was a perfect

example. Much to my dismay, he stopped hanging out with us. I figured there was something wrong with him because I had alcohol and girls at my house every single night. I had no idea who could pass up such an opportunity. He hadn't hung out with me for about three months. Adam was in film school, and he had heard about a documentary that was being released, and said we needed to go out to Burbank for an early showing. We hadn't seen each other in quite a while, and this would be our first time getting together in months.

This film was titled, *Expelled: No Intelligence Allowed*, and this movie night would be a turning point in my life. The movie forced me to question my somewhat newly found atheistic beliefs. I had been using the argument of appealing to authority, thinking that I would not have to provide any answers. I turned to atheists and agnostics such as Dr. Richard Dawkins, Dr. Michael Ruse, and other "esteemed" professors of the field to explain why everything began to exist, why things have the appearance of design but were merely a mirage rather than the truth, that there is a Creator who designed us. But the evidence pointed against such an appeal. The very professors I hoped would give me the answers I was looking for only came up with embarrassing theories.

Dr. Michael Ruse argued that all life formed on the backs of crystals. Richard Dawkins surmised that maybe an intelligent life form, which also came about by means of Darwinian evolution, left a seed here on Earth that eventually became the human race. That theory is known as panspermia—a fancy way of saying that *aliens* did it. It was easy to see the goalpost was simply being moved, and the best of the best, the most antagonistic atheists who I had hoped could explain these fundamental questions about life, sounded like they knew less than I did when the simplest of questions were asked.

I didn't leave the film screening as a Christian, but I did leave as an agnostic with my own beliefs and a sincere doubt that atheism would supply the answers to my questions. After the film, I looked online for people who could answer the questions that those men couldn't. But I came to the conclusion there was a reason they couldn't, and that reason would become quite frightening when I considered the ramifications at my next visit with Adam.

THREE DAYS BEFORE MY PERSONAL RESURRECTION

Shortly after the new year, Adam reached out again. He said he wanted to get back in shape and wondered if I wanted to start going to the gym. I agreed thinking it would be nice to hang out with my friend who had previously been missing-in-action. But before we made it to the gym, we launched into a conversation about life.

I knew he was going to church because he would come to my work on Sunday between the morning service at his home church and the college-based Bible study he attended. The Bible study took place at the church connected to the parking lot of the restaurant where I worked. But he explained the church he had started attending was quite different from the one I had visited when I decided to become an atheist. Adam said that at his new church you couldn't sleep around and get drunk without someone sharing the reason those behaviors were not okay. He made it clear that the congregation cared enough about people that they didn't want them walking in wickedness and thinking they were still in God's grace. I told him I thought that was crazy. However, I admitted it made more sense than simply going out and doing whatever you wanted without God having an impact on your moral inclinations.

That discussion led to talking about the afterlife, in which Adam asked me about my relationship with God, and whether I thought I would be going to heaven when I died. I told him I definitely would because I was a good person. He then asked me if I would be okay with him testing me to see if I truly was good enough to get into Heaven. The exchange went something like this:

The Good Person Test

Adam: "How many lies have you told in your whole life?"
Me: "I don't know - too many to count."
Adam: "What do you call someone who has told so many lies that they can't even count them?"
Me: "A liar."
Adam: "Have you ever taken anything that didn't belong to you, regardless of value?"
Me: "Of course I have. Hasn't everyone?"
Adam: "Last one, and I remind you, I've only asked you two of the ten questions I had in mind. Have you ever stubbed

your toe or been really angry or disgusted and yelled out, Oh my G*d?"

Me: "I probably have. A couple of times."

Adam explained, "You see, God gave you life, breath, a tongue, and a mind to think with. When you want to showcase disgust and contempt, you use his name to do so. You don't say 'Oh my Adolf Hitler!' or 'My Mussolini' or 'My Joseph Stalin.' You show disgust by using the name of the One who made you, lived, and died for you. It's really serious; it's the sin of blasphemy. So you are..."

Me: "A blasphemer."

Adam: "Actually no. You are a lying, thieving, blasphemer." He went on to further explain, "By your own admission—I'm not judging you—but by your own admission, you are a lying, thieving, blasphemer. If you stood before God on the day of judgment and were judged by those standards, would you be found innocent or guilty?"

I responded, "Well, if He judged me by those standards, I guess I would be guilty."

He continued, "So, would you go to heaven or hell?"

I admitted, "If those are the standards, then I would go to hell."

He asked, "Does that concern you?"

I replied, "Of course it does, but..."

Adam interjected, "Do you know what God did for guilty sinners so they wouldn't have to spend eternity in hell getting the judgment that they deserve? Two thousand years ago, Jesus Christ died a horrible death on a rugged cross on Calvary's hill.

When Jesus Christ died, the judgment of God and the love of God met directly in the center of a cross, which the Romans made to provide Jesus the most excruciating pain.

Second Corinthians chapter 5, verse 21 says, *"For our sake he made him to be sin who knew no sin, so that in him we might become the righteousness of God."* Jesus was treated as a criminal and paid the penalty for the sins committed by every human who ever lived and who would ever live. When He was dying in agony on the cross, He cried out a word "Tetelestai," which was an accounting term that would be stamped on a piece of paper when a debt had been fully paid. Jesus said "paid in full" because He had paid for the sins of the world, completely and finally on the cross. Now all you need to do is repent, which means to turn away from the sinful ways of the world and place your trust completely in Christ. When God sees you on the day of judgment, He will not see "Chad Davidson—guilty sinner," He will see his Son, Jesus Christ, who has already paid for your sins. You just place your complete trust in Him, accept the gift of salvation, and trust that His shed blood has covered your sins. When are you going to do that?"

And I said, "Not right now."

THEY SOLD THEIR SOULS FOR ROCK-N-ROLL

I wasn't ready to surrender yet, but as Adam and I were to head to the gym to strike up a conversation with someone about music, I was only going to last a little longer as a non-believer.

Now, I was a massive fan of any music that was hard. Bands

like Hatebreed, Devil Driver, Throwdown, and Otep were the ones I listened to on a regular basis and had even seen live. But my favorite band at that time was a band that was the catalyst for my love of metal—Slipknot. I studied their lyrics thoroughly with my friends. I printed out all their lyrics and read them instead of whatever was going on in Mr. Hixon's ninth grade science class (and I still don't know). I would sing songs like "Heretic Anthem," and "Wait and Bleed," which had lyrics that said, "Like a dead beat winner, I wanna be a sinner. If you're five-five-five, then I'm a six-six-six. What's it like to be a heretic?" Then there's the song that said, "Everything is 3D blasphemy," and another song that said, "Contagion, I'm sitting here at the side of Satan."

At the time, I didn't think much of those lyrics. I figured it was just showmanship. So, when Adam and his friend started talking about how the Beatles were satanic, I thought, "Dude, you guys must be wild. I listen to satanic bands, and the Beatles just sing that all you need is love." I mocked the idea, but little did I know that conversation would be the impetus I needed to make me just curious enough to watch a video Adam would give to me.

He said, "You don't have to believe me, but I'll give you a video when we get back home." I honestly didn't think much about it, and I took the video, and went home. I didn't watch it that night, but the next night, while I was at a going away party, I asked another friend if he wanted to watch it with me sometime. I said, "Hey man, I got this weird video about music and you're more spiritual than I am. Do you want to check it out?"

He said yes, and on January 18th, 2009, I drove over to his house with the video.

I didn't go there with the expectation of my life changing that night. I went to hang out with a friend, watch an interesting video, and probably go out and drink after. When I arrived at his house, we talked about the events of the previous night, and how he ran his dad's car into the brick wall in front of the house. I told him I didn't even know how I got home that night, but my car was parked in its usual spot, and I was asleep in my bed without remembering much.

We eventually got around to watching the video, which continued to weigh on me. It detailed the history of music and how so many of the world's most prominent musicians were followers of a Satanist by the name of Aleister Crowley. It talked about John Lennon of the Beatles, saying that his entire philosophy matched the maxim of the 19th-century occultist – "Do What Thou Wilt" - which reigned supreme over anything else. It explained how so many artists engaged in automatic writing, in which lyrics are downloaded into their minds from an outside source. Bands like The Doors, Jimi Hendrix, Led Zeppelin, The Rolling Stones, Black Sabbath, and many others have performed seances and other occult practices. Many of the musicians admitted to demonic possession, which provided them with lyrics that would captivate people for multiple eras and still captivate many to this day. By the end of the video, my friend and I couldn't get around the truth—a devil most certainly existed.

These people—separated by eras and continents and

without the aid of the internet—could not give out the exact same message—which was in direct opposition to the God of the Bible—unless there was a spirit behind it. No amount of excuses could bring me to accept that this synergy was anything other than a spiritual being. While I was presented the Gospel two days earlier, it was what was presented in this film that God used to bring me out of the dominion of darkness and into the dominion of His dear Son!

The Bible says a few things about this. In Ephesians 2:8-9, it is written: "For by grace you have been saved through faith; and that not of yourselves, it is the gift of God; not as a result of works, so that no one may boast."

And Romans 10:17 tells us: "So faith comes from hearing, and hearing by the word of Christ." The words Christ gave me in order to access the grace in which I now stand can be found in Matthew 12:30: "He who is not with Me is against Me; and he who does not gather with Me scatters."

In summary, to not make a choice is to make a choice.

I knew right then that not only was I ignorant to think I was simply a bystander in the enemy's plans, but so is anyone else who doesn't come to Christ. God's Word is clear: the enemy works through any child of disobedience who wants to do their own will over God's (Ephesians 2:2). They may think they are free in their sin, but the truth is that they are slaves to the sin that has overcome them. I knew it was true because deep down I was a slave to every single one of my sins—alcohol being the chief one.

But it was the words of Jesus that God used to break me and bring about the faith I needed to be saved.

I remember feeling guilty because of my sin. I remember taking my tongue ring out, getting on my knees, and praying for the first time. I drove from my friend's house and headed down the freeway to the beach. I repented of my sins and begged God to forgive me for neglecting so great a salvation all those years. I threw away my music and told God I was going to worship Him alone for the rest of my life! The next day, my first full day as a blood-bought believer in Christ, I bought a Bible and started reading the Gospel of Matthew. I called my friend and told him, "Bro, I don't know who made this video, but I want to meet him. I just gave my life to Christ, and I have to meet the man who was used to bring me to know Him."

He said, "Don't worry, you will meet him on Sunday. He's our pastor and we'll be going to church!"

I met Joe Schimmel that Sunday, and he became my pastor. Not long after, he began discipling me by taking me out to share the Gospel on the streets of Santa Monica. I also fell in love with a beautiful woman who went with us. After some much-needed sanctification, I sat down with Pastor Schimmel to talk about her—not only because he was my pastor but because the girl I had fallen in love with was also his daughter. I told him my intentions and said the next time we had a talk like this, it would be to ask for her hand in marriage.

We got married on April 14th, 2012, and our firstborn son arrived nine months and five days from our wedding day. His name is Eliezer Chad Davidson, and he is the first of four children. My wife and I have two boys and two girls: Eliezer Chad, Justus Irenaeus, Ariella Moriah, and Galilee Grace. I have not only been blessed enough to have four fantastic children and an amazing wife, but I've been serving at my church as a youth leader since 2012, and I have worked with Good Fight Ministries since 2013. I now serve Jesus by helping lead others to Christ through the ministry and the minister who brought me to the Lord!

CHAPTER 4
DISCIPLESHIP IN THE EARLY CHURCH

> "...the Church, having received this preaching and this faith, although scattered throughout the whole world, yet, as if occupying but one house, carefully preserves it."
> **– Irenaeus of Lyon**

When wrestling with discipleship, one crucial aspect involves examining the lessons of the past and striving to learn from them. In this chapter, we will delve into the post-apostolic era of the Church's efforts in discipleship, as well as, some examples of discipleship during the Early Church period. As we explore the methodologies employed by the Church in this era, it's imperative to glean wisdom from various sources while also identifying potential deviations from Holy Scripture. The significance of evaluating all things against God's Word cannot be overstated. With this said, we will look to this transitional period from the time of the apostles to their predecessors to see how God worked mightily through the Church in growing people through discipleship.

Transitioning from an assistant coach position to head coach, my aspiration was to combine the wisdom imparted to me by the two head coaches under whose tutelage I had the privilege of enjoying during my high school years. I was determined to infuse my wrestlers with a blend of the stringent, structured approach of the disciplined obedience instilled by coach Paul Mole. Coach Mole was my head coach for the first three years of my high school career. Simultaneously, I endeavored to challenge my athletes by pitting them against top-tier opponents in the most demanding tournaments.

Richard Carillo, who assumed coaching responsibilities in my senior year, emphasized the significance of high-caliber competition. This helped us reach the next level. Because of this foundation, I made the choice to lead my team to national tournaments and the best competitions in our area. By assimilating and incorporating valuable elements from each coach's philosophy, my wrestlers were able to swiftly ascend to a remarkably competitive level, even though most of them had very little to no experience coming into high school. This underscores the benefits of attaining wisdom from those who came before us and paved our way through their diligent efforts. The result of gathering the wisdom of many counselors, and applying as much of that wisdom to benefit those who are under our care, is far-reaching.

Like the coaching tree concept in football or the coach-to-athlete connection in wrestling, the relationship between one who disciples and a disciple is of prime importance. This becomes evident when we turn our gaze to discipleship in the early days of the church. An in-depth examination of the developing church reveals a lineage including figures like Irenaeus, who was a direct disciple of Polycarp, who received guidance from the Apostle John. These unbroken connections to the apostolic era beautifully illustrate the continuity of the church adhering to the truths spoken by Jesus and declaring the Church's resilience against the onslaught of their inevitable challenges. Irenaeus put it in this way concerning the church's consistent message:

> "The church, though dispersed throughout the whole world, even to the ends of the earth, has received from the apostles and their disciples this faith: [She believes] in one God, the Father Almighty, Maker of heaven, and earth, and the sea, and all things that are in them; and in one Christ Jesus, the Son of God, who became incarnate for our salvation; and in the Holy Spirit, who proclaimed through the prophets the dispensations of God, and the advents, and the birth from a virgin, and the passion, and the resurrection from the dead, and the ascension into heaven in the flesh of the beloved Christ Jesus, our Lord, and His [future] manifestation from heaven in the glory of the Father "to gather all things in one."
> 1

Irenaeus further explained that no matter the region,

because of the teachings of the Scriptures, we have the same doctrines regardless of the culture in which it is found:

> "For the Churches which have been planted in Germany do not believe or hand down anything different, nor do those in Spain, nor those in Gaul, nor those in the East, nor those in Egypt, nor those in Libya, nor those which have been established in the central regions of the world. But as the sun, that creature of God, is one and the same throughout the whole world, so also the preaching of the truth shines everywhere, and enlightens all men that are willing to come to a knowledge of the truth."

So, how did the early church do this without being able to tweet, text, or even send an email? While I would never want to limit the Holy Spirit and His role in keeping the Church from becoming part of the world, we can recognize how God used His Church to bring people into a relationship with Christ and into fellowship with true Christian believers. One of the methods used by the early church for discipleship was through creeds. They were used not only in the Post-Apostolic era but also during the Apostolic age where many passages of Scripture were originally given in a spoken creedal form to the Church (e.g., 1 Corinthians 15:3-8; Philippians 2:6-11). This was not only because of the necessity of keeping oral maxims in a culture where many were illiterate but to keep the essential truths at the forefront of the Church's mind. This practice continued in the era after the apostles and is best explained by

St. Cyril of Jerusalem in the latter part of the fourth century when he emphasized the need for creeds and how they convey the story of the Bible to those who cannot afford to read it.

> *"But in learning the Faith and in professing it, acquire and keep that only which is now delivered to you by the Church, and which has been built up strongly out of all the Scriptures. For since all cannot read the Scriptures, some being hindered as to the knowledge of them by want of learning, and others by a lack of leisure, in order that the soul may not perish from ignorance, we comprise the whole doctrine of the Faith in a few lines. This summary I wish you both to commit to memory when I recite it, and to rehearse it with all diligence among yourselves, not writing it out on paper but engraving it by memory upon your heart, taking care while you rehearse it that no Catechumen chance to overhear the things which have been delivered to you. I wish you also to keep this as a provision through the whole course of your life and beside this to receive no other, neither if we ourselves should change and contradict our present teaching, nor if an adverse angel, transformed into an angel of light should wish to lead you astray (2 Corinthians 11:14). For though we or an angel from heaven preach to you any other gospel than that you have received, let him be to you anathema (Galatians 1:8-9). So, for the present listen while I simply say the Creed and commit it to memory; but at the proper season, expect the confirmation out of Holy Scripture of each part of the contents. For the articles of the Faith were not composed as seemed good to men; but the most important points collected out of all the Scripture*

> *make up one complete teaching of the Faith. And just as the mustard seed in one small grain contains many branches, so also this Faith has embraced in few words all the knowledge of godliness in the Old and New Testaments. Take heed then, brethren, and hold fast the traditions which you now receive, and write them on the table of your heart."*[2]

The ultimate goal of this approach is for Scripture to be wholly written onto the "table of your heart." Certain means are to be used to help us grow in our faith and understand what we believe. It is the goal of anyone engaging in discipleship to make sure they clearly explain the tenets of the Christian faith to those who have come into relationship with Christ. We should be "teaching them all" that Jesus has commanded us (Matthew 28:18-20). By doing this and expressing what is required, we will help our brothers or sisters grow in their faith and in their understanding of the call to discipleship of every believer. We will be a part of the sanctification process as we see them grow more and more like Jesus Christ.

How did this practice of creedal understanding and the teachings of Christ affect the early Christians? We are given not only letters written about the Christians in their lifetime from men like Pliny the Younger, a magistrate of Rome in the early second century, but we also see how early Christians describe their behavior while writing to one another. A great representation of what the Church should look like to the world is found in an epistle of Mathetes to Diognetus, which gives us a vivid description of Christians and their position in the world:

"For the Christians are distinguished from other men neither by country, nor language, nor the customs which they observe. For they neither inhabit cities of their own, nor employ a peculiar form of speech, nor lead a life which is marked out by any singularity. The course of conduct which they follow has not been devised by any speculation or deliberation of inquisitive men; nor do they, like some, proclaim themselves the advocates of any merely human doctrines. But, inhabiting Greek as well as barbarian cities, according as the lot of each of them has determined and following the customs of the natives in respect to clothing, food, and the rest of their ordinary conduct, they display to us their wonderful and confessedly striking method of life. They dwell in their own countries but simply as sojourners. As citizens, they share in all things with others and yet endure all things as if foreigners. Every foreign land is to them as their native country, and every land of their birth as a land of strangers. They marry, as do all [others]; they beget children; but they do not destroy their offspring. They have a common table, but not a common bed. They are in the flesh, but they do not live after the flesh (2 Corinthians 10:3). They pass their days on earth, but they are citizens of heaven (Philippians 3:20). They obey the prescribed laws and at the same time surpass the laws by their lives. They love all men and are persecuted by all. They are unknown and condemned; they are put to death and restored to life (2 Corinthians 6:9). They are poor yet make many rich (2 Corinthians 6:10); they are in lack of all things, and yet abound in all; they are dishonored, and yet in their very dishonor are glorified. They are evil spoken of, and yet are justi-

fied; they are reviled, and bless (2 Corinthians 4:12); they are insulted and repay the insult with honor; they do good, yet are punished as evildoers. When punished, they rejoice as if quickened into life; they are assailed by the Jews as foreigners and are persecuted by the Greeks; yet those who hate them are unable to assign any reason for their hatred."[3]

"To sum up all in one word — what the soul is in the body, Christians are in the world. The soul is dispersed through all the members of the body, and Christians are scattered through all the cities of the world. The soul dwells in the body yet is not of the body; and Christians dwell in the world, yet are not of the world. The invisible soul is guarded by the visible body, and Christians are known indeed to be in the world, but their godliness remains invisible. The flesh hates the soul, and wars against it, (1Peter 2:11) though itself suffering no injury, because it is prevented from enjoying pleasures; the world also hates the Christians, though in nowise injured, because they abjure pleasures. The soul loves the flesh that hates it, and [loves also] the members; Christians likewise love those that hate them. The soul is imprisoned in the body yet keeps together that very body; and Christians are confined in the world as in a prison, and yet they keep together the world. The immortal soul dwells in a mortal tabernacle; and Christians dwell as sojourners in corruptible [bodies], looking for an incorruptible dwelling in the heavens. The soul, when but ill-provided with food and drink, becomes better; in like manner, the Christians, though subjected day by day to punishment, increase the more in number. God has

assigned them this illustrious position, which it were unlawful for them to forsake."[4]

Let these early Christians facing legitimate persecution be an encouragement to us. Let the wisdom they share fall on listening ears that want to receive the wisdom that comes from those who have walked with Christ and are now with Him in glory!

CHAPTER 5
DISCIPLESHIP THROUGH GOD'S WORD

"Wherefore I exhort and entreat you all, disregard what this man and that man thinks about these things and inquire from the Scriptures all these things; and having learnt what are the true riches, let us pursue after them that we may obtain also the eternal good things."
–John Chrysostom

ONE NIGHT at wrestling camp before my junior season, Coach John Acevedo, a former Olympian, gathered all of us wrestlers to watch a Division 1 wrestler's tape, analyzing their tendencies, strengths, and weaknesses. This taught us the art of scouting opponents and crafting strategies to defeat them, something I hadn't considered before. Little did I know this skill would prove to be even more valuable when I became a coach than what it did for me as a wrestler. As an assistant coach, I discovered that platforms like YouTube and "Flowrestling" allowed me to watch nearly every match of our upcoming opponents, helping me create effective game plans for my wrestlers.

While this is a great way to gain an advantage, it is usually only beneficial when the opponents are on a somewhat level playing field. Sometimes, when you watch two wrestlers step onto the mat, you find that their skill levels may not be as close as you first thought. This became evident when one of my wrestlers was set to face our crosstown rival's top wrestler in the CIF Finals. Our soon-to-be opponent had been on a winning streak, and both wrestlers had advanced to the finals. I had scouted the opponent thoroughly, understanding his strengths, particularly his cross-face cradle on top and a formidable single-leg takedown that set up his entire neutral game, and I believed I had developed a strong game plan to counter his strategies.

Though shorter for his weight class, my wrestler possessed immense strength, a 145-pound athlete bench pressing over 300 pounds. We focused on a technique known as a "Club and Dig" in hopes of countering his patented single-leg takedown. Our strategy emphasized initiating the technique immediately as the match began, with my wrestler clubbing his neck right from the whistle and swiftly getting into the underhook position.

In my mind, we had it all figured out; this underhook should thwart any attempt at the single-leg, and then we could begin to set the tone of the match as we would then be able to impose our will onto the match. However, our opponent saw things differently. He remained undeterred, displaying unwavering confidence in his abilities. He effortlessly bypassed our defenses, wrestling through them as if facing a junior varsity competitor. Despite our meticulous preparation and my wrestler's incredible strength, this young man's single leg proved unstoppable, resulting in his straightforward victory.

Sometimes, the outcome of a contest doesn't favor you because your opponent possesses something that you couldn't have anticipated or for which you couldn't adequately prepare. I could relate this to how the Sadducees must have felt when Jesus dismantled their favorite argument against the afterlife.

I'm going to be honest with you - I love debate. I love watching formal debates, and I enjoy mixing it up with anyone who disagrees with me. Whether traditional or informal, expressing ideas openly with those whose ideas may differ allows us to plead our case in a way that enables us to sharpen our arguments. This is also something the rabbis did long before God became a man in the person of Jesus Christ. In fact, the Pharisees and Sadducees of Jesus' day had been engaging in the debate of whether there is an afterlife or not for centuries. It seems that the Sadducees had an argument they had been presenting to which the Pharisees could not supply a sufficient reply. Therefore, they felt they had a knockdown, drag-out argument disproving the Pharisees' belief that there is an afterlife.

An ancient non-biblical proverb suggests, "The enemy of my enemy is my friend." And that seems to be what was happening in Matthew 22. The Pharisees and Sadducees, who weren't all that kind to one another, teamed up to come after Jesus intellectually. However, this proved futile and somewhat embarrassing for both, as Jesus continued to refute them with Scripture. But this proved to be a very important exchange, not only because they did not even bother challenging Jesus theologically after this, but how Jesus answered them also shows us the high level of respect Jesus was given concerning His knowledge of Scripture. Thus, if we are going to be followers of Jesus, we need to have the same high regard for Scripture that He held. If we are being honest, no person can claim to be a follower of Christ and deviate from Jesus' view on the afterlife since that would mean they are simply followers of themselves and not of Christ! Matthew chapter 22, verses 23-33 reads:

> *"On that day some of Sadducees (who say there is no resurrection) came to Jesus and questioned Him, asking, "Teacher, Moses said, 'If a man dies having no children, his brother as next of kin shall marry his wife, and raise up children for his brother.' Now there were seven brothers with us; and the first married and died, and having no children left his wife to his brother; so also, the second, and the third, down to the seventh. Last of all, the woman died. In the resurrection, therefore, whose wife of the seven will she be? For they all had married her." But Jesus answered and said to them, "You are mistaken, not understanding the scriptures nor the power of God. For in the resurrection, they neither marry nor are given in marriage, but are like angels in heaven. But regarding the resurrection of the dead, have you not read what was spoken to you by God: 'I am the God of Abraham, and the God of Isaac, and the God of Jacob'? He is not the God of the dead but of the*

living." When the crowds heard this, they were astonished at His teaching."

When correctly applied, this argument exposes a person's answers as absurd. From their perspective, if Jesus claimed she was married to all of them, He would seemingly endorse polygamy. However, God's design is clear. Man is to be united in marriage to one spouse (Matthew 19:5; Genesis 2:23-24), and Jesus couldn't endorse such an absurd notion. On the other hand, if Jesus stated she was married to some of the men but not to others, it would potentially provide grounds for divorce without Biblical justification. Jesus not only rebuked them by bluntly stating, "You are mistaken, not understanding the Scriptures," but He also demonstrated that their argument rested on a logical fallacy known as the "False dilemma" or "Either/or fallacy."

This fallacy occurs when someone erroneously asserts that there are only two possible options or sides in an argument when, in reality, there are more. Jesus made it evident that there was a third option beyond the limited choices presented by the Sadducees and revealed the true nature of the situation. What's particularly noteworthy is that Jesus didn't stop there. He provided a compelling argument for the concept of the afterlife, utilizing a verb tense. Furthermore, he carefully selected a scripture passage that would be accepted by the Sadducees within their understanding of the written text of Scripture.

Jesus skillfully employed a concept Paul spoke about when he told believers, "I have become all things to all men, so that I may by all means save some" (1 Corinthians 9:22). He avoided allowing the Sadducees to claim the prophets may have been speaking allegorically about the afterlife. Instead, He focused on what they would have understood as a literal interpretation of the Scriptures. In doing so, He effectively bypassed this argument by appealing to that which they would readily accept.

The Pulpit Commentary describes it this way:

"To our minds, Jesus, might have adduced stronger arguments from other books of Scripture, e.g. Isaiah, Ezekiel, and Daniel; but the Sadducees had drawn their objection from the Pentateuch, therefore from that section of the Bible, He refutes them. To the books of Moses was always made the ultimate appeal in confirmation of doctrine; in the supreme authority of these writings all sects agreed. The utterances of the prophets were explained away as allegorical, poetical, and rhetorical; the plain, historical statements of the Law could not at that time be thus treated. Christ endorses unreservedly the Divine inspiration of the Pentateuch; he intimates that it was the voice of God to all time, and providentially directed to disperse such errors as those now produced."[1]

Not only does Jesus use the books the Sadducees would have accepted, but He also makes His entire appeal from the tense of a verb! Jesus' knockdown, drag-out case for the afterlife comes from the fact that when God said to Moses at the burning bush, "I AM the God of Abraham, Isaac and Jacob," all of these patriarchs had passed away, but He was currently (I

AM...not I was) the God of Abraham, Isaac and Jacob because they were currently with him!

The Cambridge Bible for Schools and Colleges puts it this way: "the argument for the Resurrection is inferred. For if the patriarchs are living, they are living in [...] and therefore they are awaiting a resurrection; cp. Hebrews 11:16."[2]

If Jesus had such regard for Scripture, that the tense of the verb matters, how can we sit and let this Word collect dust on our shelves or remain buried somewhere between the other apps we leave unopened?

It is through God's Word we see our own reflection, and through His law, we recognize our own imperfections in our conquest of becoming like our Savior. James chapter 1 verses 23-25 says, *"For if anyone is a hearer of the word and not a doer, he is like a man who looks at his natural face in a mirror; for once he has looked at himself and gone away, he has immediately forgotten what kind of person he was. But one who looks intently at the perfect law, the law of liberty, and abides by it, not having become a forgetful hearer but an effectual doer, this man will be blessed in what he does."*

It is also through His Word that we see how we are to live. *"How can a young man keep his way pure? By keeping it according to your word"* (Psalm 119:9).

When I consider the many key aspects of growing in our relationship with Christ, there are very few as paramount as the place in our hearts that we give to the word of God, the respect we have for the authority that God's Word holds over our lives. Not only does the Word of God act as the final authority concerning doctrine and the way of life, but it also outlines the means of sanctification that Jesus prescribed for His disciples. *"Sanctify them in the truth; Your word is truth"* (John 17:17).

The barometer Jesus set for us to determine truth is the Word by which God has spoken. It is the very means that God uses—through the power of the Holy Spirit, to make us more like Jesus. Why would Jesus place such a lofty task upon the Word that we have received? Because the word contains more than just platitudes, stories, and philosophy. The words of Scripture come directly from God Himself: *"All Scripture is inspired by God and profitable for teaching, for reproof, for correction, for training in righteousness"* (2 Timothy 3:16).

The original Greek term that is translated "inspired by God" is given a far greater description when the original language used by Paul is "unpacked." As commentator Albert Barnes notes:

> *"Is given by inspiration of God - All this is expressed in the original by one word - Θεόπνευστος Theopneustos. This word occurs nowhere else in the New Testament. It properly means, God-inspired - from Θεός Theos, "God," and πνέω pneō, "to breathe, to breathe out." The idea of "breathing upon, or breathing into the soul," is that which the word naturally conveys. Thus, God breathed into the nostrils of Adam the breath of life Genesis 2:7, and thus the Saviour breathed on his disciples, and said, "receive ye the Holy Ghost" (John 20:22). The idea seems to have been, that the life was in the breath, and that an intelligent spirit was communicated with the breath."*[3]

Understanding the significance of the Word of God, which is considered divinely inspired, becomes clear through both Jesus and His apostles. Peter, when describing the miraculous event he saw when Moses and Elijah were on a mount and heard the voice of God, emphasizes the point that the Bible is more reliable than such experiences. He encourages us to view it as our guiding light in the darkness of life.

> *"For we did not follow cleverly devised tales when we made known to you the power and coming of our Lord Jesus Christ, but we were eyewitnesses of his majesty. For when he received honor and glory from God the Father, such an utterance as this was made to him by the Majestic Glory, "This is my beloved son with whom I am well-pleased"— and we ourselves heard this utterance made from heaven when we were with him on the holy mountain. So, we have the prophetic word made surer, to which you do well to pay attention as to a lamp shining in a dark place, until the day dawns and the morning star arises in your hearts. But know this first of all, that no prophecy of Scripture is a matter of one's own interpretation, for no prophecy was ever made by an act of human will, but men moved by the Holy Spirit spoke from God."* (2 Peter 1:16-21).

The Bible is described as the "imperishable seed" in First Peter chapter 1, verses 23-25: *"For you have been born again, not of seed which is perishable but imperishable, that is, through the living and enduring word of God. For, 'All flesh is like grass, And all its glory like the flower of grass. The grass withers, And the flower falls off, But the word of the Lord endures forever.' And this is the word which was preached to you."*

According to James, this imperishable seed can "save your souls" when received with humility (James 1:21). As Paul advised Timothy, these words, when combined with faith, have the power to lead us to salvation: *"...from childhood you have known the sacred writings which are able to give you the wisdom that leads to salvation through faith which is in Christ Jesus."* (2 Timothy 3:15).

The New Testament makes this clear, and the Old Testament also provides numerous texts illustrating the profound impact of God's Word on our spiritual well-being when applied to our lives. The very first Psalm in the book of Psalms, serves as a preface to all 150 chapters of this book of the Bible. It presents two distinct individuals with contrasting destinies: the blessed man and the wicked man. Their primary distinction lies in what they meditate upon and with whom they choose to associate.

> *"How blessed is the man who does not walk in the counsel of the wicked, Nor stand in the path of sinners, Nor sit in the seat of scoffers! But his delight is in the law of the Lord, And in His law, he meditates day and night. He will be like a tree firmly planted by streams of water, which yields its fruit in its season And its leaf does not wither; And in whatever he does, he prospers. The wicked are not so, but they are like chaff which the wind drives away. Therefore, the wicked will not stand in the judgment, Nor sinners in the assembly of the righteous. For the*

Lord knows the way of the righteous, But the way of the wicked will perish" (Psalm 1:1-6).

The blessed man meditates on God's Word and, because of this, becomes rooted and bears fruit. But not so with the wicked. Not only do they avoid meditating upon God's Word, they also associate with bad company, which corrupts good morals and seem to progressively go in the wrong direction. Adam Clarke provides the following commentary: "He who walks according to the counsel of the ungodly will soon:

1. Stand to look on the wage of sinners; and thus, being off his guard, he will soon be a partaker in their evil deeds.
2. He who has abandoned himself to transgression will, in all probability, soon become hardened by the deceitfulness of sin; and sit down with the scorner, and endeavor to turn religion into ridicule.

The last connection we find is:

1. The seat answers to the sitting of the scornful.
2. The way answers to the standing of the sinner; and
3. The counsel answers to the walking of the ungodly.

The great lesson to be learned from the passage is that sin is progressive; one evil propensity or act leads to another. He who acts by bad counsel may soon do evil deeds, and he who abandons himself to evil doings may end his life in total apostasy from God. 'When lust has conceived, it brings forth sin; and when sin is finished, it brings forth death.' Solomon, the son of David, adds a profitable advice to those words of his father: 'Enter not into the path of the wicked, and go not in the way of evil men; avoid it, pass not by it, turn from it, and pass away.'"[4]

Psalm 1 serves as an introductory guide to understanding all 150 Psalms. But the longest chapter—Psalm 119—reinforces the central importance of God's word using synonyms and repetition. Notably, this chapter was a favorite of William Wilberforce, the renowned abolitionist dedicated to ending slavery in England. Dr. J. Vernon McGee mentioned this in his "Thru the Bible" commentary introduction to the Psalm. Dr. McGee notes: "William Wilberforce, the statesman who was converted in the Wesleyan movement, wrote in his diary, 'Walked from Hyde Park corner, repeating the 119th Psalm in great comfort.' What a wonderful statement. If you can't sleep at night, don't count sheep; count the letters of the Hebrew alphabet and read verses of this psalm. It would mean a great deal to you."[5]

Dr. McGee references the Hebrew alphabet because the chapter is 176 verses comprising 22 stanzas with 8 verses per stanza. Each of the 22 stanzas correlate to a letter of the Hebrew alphabet. It appears the author of Psalm 119 wanted us to know that every letter, and therefore word, that we read or speak should relate to the Word of God. As it states in Second Corinthians chapter 10, verse 5: "... *we are taking every thought captive to the obedience of Christ.*"

When put into application and practice, Psalm 119 verse 11 summarizes everything the Psalmist was attempting to express in the book of Psalms: *"Your word I have treasured in my heart, That I may not sin against You."*

Let this be true of us!

Hide God's Word in your heart and live in a manner worthy of the calling you have received. Let God wrestle your desires down as you take them captive to the Word of God. You cannot begin to disciple others or even be discipled yourself if you do not know God's Word. If you do not allow His Word to take precedence in your life, you will be taken captive by the wind or every other doctrine that comes around. Trust in His word and watch God use His word to establish and edify you in your walk with Christ!

CHAPTER 6
DISCIPLESHIP THROUGH THE FEAR OF THE LORD

> "For this reason, righteousness and peace are now far departed from you, inasmuch as everyone abandons the fear of God, and is become blind in his faith, neither walks in the laws of his commandments."
> **–Clement of Rome**

My first wrestling coach was a stern-faced Marine. My brothers had warned me that he didn't put up with any nonsense. I was told and discovered on my own that if I was going to be a wrestler, I needed to shut up, listen, and follow the coach's lead. There was no doubt this is a healthy way of leadership in a wrestling room, and it's precisely what was needed for a group of wrestlers who were born athletes. But having just decided to commit to the sport of wrestling while in high school, it was also very intimidating.

We had a couple of guys with some experience, but twelve of the fourteen weight classes were going to be manned by wrestlers who had never stepped on a mat before walking into high school. This was true for me, and if we were going to reach our goals, we needed a strong coach who could show us exactly what would be required. He also needed to keep us in line if we were going to reach a modicum of the potential that so many of us showed.

The first couple of years served as a "feeling out" process. I knew Coach was tough in the gym, but I got to know him better off the mat when I took his history class. You see, I've always been an eager, gifted learner, but I was a terrible student when dealing with my teachers. I would pass my classes because I could read quickly and understand the concepts. Which meant I didn't see a need to show up for class or even do a lot of what I considered "busy work." I was also able to memorize things easily, and I used my deductive reasoning to answer test questions at a highly proficient rate. My coach soon realized I knew the material, and I did just enough to get by, but that wasn't going to be good enough in Coach's history class.

Why?

Because I had a healthy fear when it came to my coach. However, fear was not the only feeling I had regarding my coach.

When I began to take wrestling more seriously in my sophomore year of high school, I also started spending time with him outside of practice. I would go to his classroom during lunch and practice early to help clean the wrestling mats. I wanted him to know I was serious about getting better, and I wanted him to see my progression during the off-season. I got to experience a much different side of him, but it never changed the respect and fear I had for him as my coach. In fact, the reverence I feel for him will always be firmly rooted in my mind. To this day, I still refer to him as Coach Molé, and that will always be the case.

If I'm honest with myself, I knew that I needed a coach who would lay into me when I didn't remember to bring my shoes to my first varsity tournament (yes, that happened). But I also needed a coach who would present me to my class when I had accomplished the biggest upset at league finals and was named Athlete of the Week. True reverence and fear, when they occur in a relationship, lead to a healthy bond between coach and wrestler. The same can also be said about the reverence and fear we feel when we come into a proper relationship with the Lord our God.

No genuine relationship with God leads people to believe they are on the same footing as their Creator. But we serve a God who according to Isaiah, chapter 57, verse 15, is the "high and exalted one." But He will also dwell with "the contrite and lowly of spirit in order to revive the spirit of the lowly and to revive the heart of the contrite."

God always showcases the relationship we need most...*when* we need it the most, not when we *think* we need it most. His guidance is far better than any coach-to-athlete relationship could ever be, and He will never lead us to anything other than victory (Romans 8:37). However, it is impossible to have a proper relationship with God that does not also include a healthy *fear* of God. There are many who believe we don't need to fear the Lord under the New Testament, but as I will present through God's Word, that view or assumption is incorrect.

One of the key elements in what is known as the "wisdom literature" in the Old Testament is the fear of the Lord. It is illustrated in the story of Job, is the culmination of the book of Ecclesiastes, and is the essence of the book of Proverbs. These books give us wisdom and insight by way of story, adages, and psalms. There are two categories of wisdom literature, didactic and devotional, and they are as follows:

DIDACTIC LITERATURE:

1. Ecclesiastes
2. Proverbs
3. Job

DEVOTIONAL LITERATURE:

1. Psalms
2. Song of Songs
3. Lamentations

While all these books give us valuable wisdom and insight, the book of Proverbs is the one that teaches us the most regarding the fear of the Lord through proverbial pronouncements rather than story (e.g., Job). In the preamble of the book, the author explains his intent for writing in such a way: *"The fear of the Lord is the beginning of knowledge but fools despise wisdom and instruction"* (Proverbs 1:7), and *"The fear of the Lord is the beginning of wisdom, and the knowledge of the Holy One is insight"* (Proverbs 9:10).

Before we can begin to understand knowledge and gain any wisdom, we must realize that it all starts with the fear of the Lord.

In scholar Tremper Longman's book, *The Fear of the Lord is Wisdom*, he provides three types of wisdom that are gained from the book of Proverbs:

1. Practical
2. Ethical
3. Theological

While the argument can, should, and will be made that these three distinctions are interwoven, it is also important to explain the differences to see how they are used in this book.

The practical lessons of Proverbs can be found easily when we see there is a practical wisdom that, if followed closely, will bring forth a benefit or reward to anyone practicing it, even if they do not choose to fear the Lord. *"A man has joy in an apt answer, and how delightful is a timely word"* (Proverbs 15:23). This proverbial insight can benefit us practically and requires no moral standard by which we may live nor a commandment to follow. It is a statement of practical advice that those who are ready to give an answer will be a delight and joy for those who receive it.

"In all labor there is profit, but mere talk leads only to poverty" (Proverbs 14:23). Anyone can think of someone who sold them a bill of goods but could not deliver. There is practical wisdom in putting your hand to the plow and working to provide for yourself and your family. But there are still plenty of people who make plans but never plow. These practical applications, and many more, fall into a category known as a *truism*—a statement that is generally accepted as true and, therefore, repeated as such. So, does every single person who is more of a talker than a doer fall into poverty? Not necessarily. Numerous factors, both moral and immoral, may cause someone to gain wealth, and a hard laborer might actually be the one in poverty. So, the application is not true in all cases, but it is true in a vast majority. And it is solid guidance for those who listen and apply the advice.

The next category deals with the moral implications of these proverbial teachings. The ethical statements in the book of Proverbs are not commands but can carry the same weight as a command when rightly applied. According to Tremper Longman, the primary difference between a proverb and a command is that a "proverb is not universally true but true only when applied to the right situation."[1]

The ethical implications found in the book of Proverbs tend to echo many of the Ten Commandments God gave to Moses while he was on Mount Sinai. These Commandments were designed to govern God's people, and as Longman points out, the author of Proverbs seems to re-enforce six of the biblical mandates given to man. These implications also echo the commandments Jesus summarized in the New Testament as "Loving your neighbor as yourself."

They are:

1. Honor Thy Mother and Father: Proverbs 1:7, 4:1, 10:1, 13:1
2. Thou Shall Not Murder: Proverbs 1:10-12, 6:17
3. Thou Shall Not Commit Adultery: Proverbs 2:16-19, Chapter 5, 6:20-35, Chapter 7
4. Thou Shall Not Steal: Proverbs 1:13-14, 11:1
5. Thou Shall Not Bear False Witness: Proverbs 3:30, 6:18,19, 10:18, 12:17,19
6. Though Shall Not Covet: Proverbs 6:18

These ethical requirements are suitable for any standard of living in a society, but the clear indication is the author of Proverbs certainly had these requirements in mind, as well as, the third distinction of wisdom. To discuss the last of the three distinctions of wisdom–theological wisdom–we must refer back to the preamble of Proverbs and look at the foundation upon which the book is built.

"The fear of the Lord is the beginning of knowledge; but fools despise wisdom and instruction" (Proverbs 1:7).

The previous six verses of the preamble to Proverbs deal

with its practical and ethical goals, but this verse establishes the theological framework. It even states that true wisdom *begins* with the fear of the Lord. Thus, we may conclude that the other two forms of wisdom: practical and ethical, also start with the fear of the Lord.

So, what is the fear of the Lord? The definition that Longman gives is:

> *"The fear of the Lord is the sense of standing before the God who created everything, including humans, whose very existence depends on him. The emotion is approbated for wisdom because it demonstrates an acknowledgement that God is much greater than we are. Our awe of him takes our breath away and makes our knees knock together. Such a fear breeds humility and signals a willingness to receive instruction from God. Fear is not the fear that makes us run, but it is the fear that makes us pay attention and listen."*[2]

Of verse 7, The Pulpit Commentary states, *"The expression describes that reverential attitude or holy fear which man, when his heart is set aright, observes towards God."* Psalm 33 also places the idea of fear and awe in a similar light: *"Let all the earth fear the Lord; let all the inhabitants of the world stand in awe of Him"* (Psalm 33:8). Do you want to be wise – practically, ethically, and theologically? Then seek wisdom and come to know the fear of the Lord!

"If you seek her as silver, and search for her as for hidden treasures; then you will discern the fear of the Lord. And discover the knowledge of God" (Proverbs 2:4-5).

A passionate search of God's wisdom produces the fruit of fear of the Lord. In the New Testament, knowledge of the Lord is synonymous, in many cases, with saving knowledge. A proper understanding and love for the one true God brings forth salvation as one resolves to follow the Lord and seek Him while He may be found. This "knowledge" in the New Testament is akin to one of the aspects of fearing the Lord. Derek Kidner points out the following in his commentary on Proverbs:

"We may start with the motto and ask whether the 'fear' of the Lord implies anything more than a healthy respect for the Almighty. This it clearly does. In two passages, 2:5 and 9:10, it is made synonymous with the knowledge of him; and this knowledge is remarkably intimate. It is given by revelation ('out of his mouth', 2:6) and fostered by what could be called the practice of his presence, as commended in 3:6: 'In all thy ways acknowledge him', or literally, 'know him.' We are reminded of the goal of the new covenant itself ('they shall all know me'), for the 'upright are in his confidence' (3:32), i.e., his sōd, his intimate circle."[3]

Kidner goes on further to describe that this knowledge also comes alongside leaving our hopes, ambitions, and aspirations before the Lord as our "fear" of the Lord requires us to trust him in every way. He says, *"Such intercourse 'in all thy ways' implies, in addition to reverence and obedience, trust, and it is noteworthy that Proverbs, for all its emphasis on common sense, exalts faith above sagacity (3:5, 7) 'Trust in the Lord with all thine heart; and upon thine own understanding lean not; ... Be not wise in thine own eyes.'"*[4]

Fearing the Lord seemingly was a point of emphasis in the Early Church, as the disciples of the apostles wrote to churches explaining the importance of fearing God. For example, Clement of Rome, who many believe is mentioned by name in Scripture by the Apostle Paul (Philippians 4:3), wrote to the Corinthian church not long after the time of the apostles, calling them to fear Christ. He said, *"Let us fear the Lord Jesus [Christ], whose blood was given for us. Let us reverence our rulers; let us honor our elders; let us instruct our young men in the lesson of the fear of God. Let us guide our women toward that which is good."*[5]

This form of reverential fear can be found in both the Old and New Testament. Here are some examples:

1. The fear of the Lord leads to an appreciation of his character: "Great and marvelous are Your works, Lord God, the Almighty; righteous and true are Your ways, King of the nations" (Revelation 15:3).
2. The fear of the Lord leads to reverence and awe of his holiness in Revelation 15:4: "Who will not fear, O Lord, and glorify Your name? For You alone are holy; for all the nations will come and worship

before You, for Your righteous acts have been revealed."
3. To fear the Lord moves us to believe in and trust in Him: "You who fear the Lord, trust in the Lord; He is their help and their shield" (Psalm 115:11).
4. To fear the Lord is to hate evil: "The fear of the Lord is to hate evil; pride and arrogance and the evil way, and the perverted mouth, I hate" (Proverbs 8:13).

Attaining a greater understanding of the holiness of God also allows us to have a greater understanding of why we hate evil. Some people have a view of God that leaves out His holiness and only focuses on specific attributes that make it easier to cuddle with Him. During a personal interview with Dr. John Oswalt, we discussed the habit of so many who separate the God of the Old Testament from the God of the New Testament. They do so to their own detriment and get a warped view of who God really is. Dr. Oswalt stated:

"I really think that the great failure in the North American church is that we have good 'gentle Jesus meek and mild' and fail to understand that he's the son of the Holy God ... if you separate him from the Father who we come to know in the Old Testament, you are in deep trouble - you have turned him into a little friendly god who exists to take care of you. And that's a fallacy. He is the Holy God who made the world and he's come to save us [...] to recreate us in His own likeness."[6]

It's imperative to remember that when God is described in the book of Revelation, He is not described as "love, love, love," but by way of emphasis, He is worshipped as "Holy, Holy, Holy." He is the thrice holy God!

> *"And the four living creatures, each one of them having six wings, are full of eyes around and within; and day and night they do not cease to say, Holy, holy, holy is the Lord God the Almighty, who was and who is and who is to come"* (Revelation 4:8).

Notice the text says, "these living creatures...*do not <u>cease</u> to say...*". This wasn't a one-time thing with the God of the Old Testament, but a current event happening now and forever! Our God is the thrice holy God, worthy of worship, and one day every single knee will bow, and every single tongue will confess – whether in judgment or with the Lord – that Jesus Christ is Lord! This is the proper understanding of our God, who is not merely a "god" with whom you talk to only when you need something, but He is someone you can address with boldness because of the blood of Jesus that was spilled on our behalf. You can go directly to Him, not because of how awesome *you are* but because of how loving *He* is! We should praise God that He is on our side. I like the way Dr. Oswalt put it: *"If the little god who lives under your bed to answer your prayers loves you, that's no big deal. But if the God who could fry you alive by looking at you loves you, that's good news."*

Some people may get the wrong idea that this idea is only

found in the Old Testament, but that could not be further from the truth. In the New Testament, Jesus dwells in unapproachable light, and it is written in First Timothy chapter 6, verses 13-16:

> *"I charge you in the presence of God, who gives life to all things, and of Christ Jesus, who testified the good confession before Pontius Pilate, that you keep the commandment without stain or reproach until the appearing of our Lord Jesus Christ, which he will bring about at the proper time—he who is the blessed and only Sovereign, the King of kings and Lord of lords, who alone possesses immortality and dwells in unapproachable light, whom no man has seen or can see. To him be honor and eternal dominion! Amen."*

In the book of Revelation, the Apostle John describes Jesus in such terms:

> *"Then I turned to see the voice that was speaking with me. And having turned I saw seven golden lampstands; and in the middle of the lampstands, I saw one like a son of man, clothed in a robe reaching to the feet, and girded across his chest with a golden sash. His head and his hair were white like white wool, like snow; and his eyes were like a flame of fire. His feet were like burnished bronze, when it has been made to glow in a furnace, and his voice was like the sound of many waters. In His right hand He held seven stars, and out of His mouth came a*

sharp two-edged sword; and his face was like the sun shining in its strength" (Revelation 1:12-16).

What was John's reaction when He saw Jesus this way?

The Bible tells us a couple of verses down, *"When I saw Him, I fell at his feet like a dead man. And he placed his right hand on me, saying, 'Do not be afraid; I am the first and the last, and the living One; and I was dead, and behold, I am alive forevermore, and I have the keys of death and of Hades'"* (Revelation 1:17-18).

This is the God we serve! This is the God who loves us! Get comfortable with the fact that our God is a warrior God... and *He's on our side!* But doesn't perfect love cast out fear? Indeed, the Bible is clear that perfect love does, in fact, cast out fear!

> *"Whoever confesses that Jesus is the Son of God, God abides in him, and he in God. We have come to know and have believed the love which God has for us. God is love, and the one who abides in love abides in God, and God abides in him. By this, love is perfected with us, so that we may have confidence in the day of judgment; because as he is, so also are we in this world. There is no fear in love; but perfect love casts out fear, because fear involves punishment, and the one who fears is not perfected in love. We love, because he first loved us. If someone says, "I love God," and hates his brother, he is a liar; for the one who does not love his brother whom he has seen, cannot love God whom he has not seen. And this commandment we have from him, that the*

one who loves God should love his brother also" (1 John 4:15-21).

But what fear does it cast out? The fear that is cast out by perfect love is the fear of judgement, *not* the fear of the Lord! If we are in Christ, we rest in His arms, and He keeps us safe. If we put our trust in Him, we do not fear judgement because the judgement that we deserve has been placed upon Jesus when He died for us on the cross. This fear of judgement is not at all what the Bible describes as the "fear of the Lord." It is more a fear of the consequence of sin rather than the beneficial fear of the Lord that causes us to hate evil and have reverence for Him! As Alexander Maclaren states in his commentary on this verse: *"If I go to Jesus Christ as a sinful man and get his love bestowed upon me, then, as the next verse to my text says, my love springs in response to his to me, and in the measure in which that love rises in my heart will it frustrate its antagonistic dread."*[7]

The antagonistic dread the enemy wants us to experience is cast out because of the love which the Father has bestowed upon us! This does not mean we do not fear the Lord. It means we do not fear the consequences of those who would oppose our warrior King! It would be theologically incorrect to disciple others to know God and not teach them to fear Him. I've been in wrestling rooms where the coach is just "one of the guys," and engages in the same talk and behavior as his wrestlers. There is no distinction between the athlete and the coach, and as a result no respect is given. But on a proper wrestling team, everyone knows who is in charge. They know to whom they can go for guidance. They know that their coach has their best interest in mind. It is a particularly difficult situation when the head coach of a team or the manager of a job is not trusted and respected.

Trust and respect are synonymous, and if this is not established properly, failure is a guarantee. So, we need to make sure there isn't a problem with our relationship with God. We need to give the Lord the proper respect and honor, and we need to "stand in awe of Him." Solomon wrote at the end of his life: *"The conclusion, when all has been heard is this: fear God and keep his commandments, because this applies to every person. For God will bring every act to judgment, everything which is hidden, whether it is good or evil"* (Ecclesiastes 12:13-14).

CHAPTER 7
PROPER FOUNDATION: ARE YOU IN YOUR STANCE?

> "Unless we build on him, we build on changeable inclinations, short-lived desires, transitory aims, evanescent circumstances. Only the Christ who ever lives, and is ever 'the same yesterday, and today, and forever' is fit to be the foundation of lives that are to be immortal."
> **– Alexander Maclaren**

BUILDING A PROPER FOUNDATION

I STILL REMEMBER the first day I walked into a wrestling room. I was far more prepared than my peers. My older brothers had warned me of some of the trials and tribulations that would lie ahead for me in wrestling. My new coach, the retired Marine, was known for his tendency toward dry humor and a calculated lack of tolerance with anyone who would attempt to offer excuses. I knew from the matches I had watched my brothers compete in—and from the stories they had told me—that wrestling was not going to be anything like I had experienced while playing basketball, baseball, or even football. But I was ready for the challenge. I even convinced some of my friends to try it out and see if we could make some memories together. Plenty of them are long since forgotten, but I still remember the first time I walked into the place we would call home for those four years of high school. While there may be a good deal of memories that have long been forgotten, there are always characteristics, events, and features of that place that will always stick out.

What was the major one for me?

It was the aroma of that watered-down bleach emanating from an old yellow bucket and an even older yellow mat. The substance was supposed to kill any bacteria within a mile of the room. It definitely wasn't a pleasant smell, but it was one every wrestler grew accustomed to smelling.

The first day of practice was filled with running and fitness tests designed to determine who would last through the first week. It was also the day to establish the basic foundations of wrestling. If done right, these essentials would aid you throughout your wrestling career and help you defend against the many attacks you might encounter.

We usually called this portion of the training program "going through our lines of defense." During my time in the sport, and on the many whiteboards I've seen, there is typically a universal set of formations that most teams use. These are typically the main four listed:

1. Head
2. Hands
3. Forearms
4. Hips

Sometimes others were added, like tricks or funk, which would be number five, but these four were fairly common. As I began to coach, I noticed that my first line of defense was taught before I even got to the subject of lines of defense. And I realized that this primary line of defense was the determining factor that would allow any of the other lines to come into play.

For many in the church, we put together lines of defense to explain why we believe what we believe. It could be through apologetics, theology, testimonies, or even strong support systems. These lines of defense are vital in our walk with Christ and can come in handy when an attack befalls us. However, the reality is there is one line of defense we must understand and employ first in order for any of our additional defense strategies to be of benefit.

In Luke chapter 6, before Jesus describes building a proper foundation, He warns us about a poor foundation and how dangerous it is for the blind to lead the blind, as both will end up falling into a ditch (Luke 6:38-39). The goal for us is to become like our teacher, and He explains what it looks like to be discipled by a true teacher: *"A pupil is not above his teacher;*

but everyone, after he has been fully trained, will be like his teacher" (Luke 6:40).

Next, Jesus goes to great lengths to warn us about being a hypocrite and judging others while still having a beam in our own eye. He calls those who follow Him to actually resemble Him—the teacher—and not be two-faced hypocrites who judge. He calls His followers to be like Him, an ambassador for reconciliation to the Father. He then says these terrifying words to His followers: *"Why do you call Me, 'Lord, Lord' and do not do what I say?"* (Luke 6:46).

If we want to be faithful followers of our Teacher, we are commanded, even predestined, to be conformed to His image. Followers of Jesus are not going to look like they are shaped by the world; they are going to look like they are taught by Jesus and transformed by His Spirit! This is the foundation upon which Jesus tells us to build. True discipleship takes place when the pupil becomes like his teacher. How do we know that this is the actual foundation about which He is speaking? Because of the following statements:

> *"Everyone who comes to me and hears my words and acts upon them, I will show you who he is like; he is like a man building a house, who dug deep and laid a foundation on the rock, and when a flood occurred, the torrent burst against that house and could not shake it, because it had been built well. But the one who has heard and has not acted accordingly, is like a man who built a house on the ground without any foundation; and the torrent burst against it and immediately it*

collapsed, and the ruin of that house was great" (Luke 6:47-49)

Note that obedience to Jesus is first and foremost. We can't think this is merely about outward service. Many people equate service with obedience, which isn't correct. It doesn't necessarily work like that. If a person serves the homeless and shares the Gospel, but at home they defile themselves and get drunk, they are merely "white-washed tombs."

A.W. Tozer warns these are substitutes for authentic discipleship. He writes, *"Another substitute for discipleship I would mention (though these do not exhaust the list) is zealous religious activity. Working for Christ has today been accepted as the ultimate test of godliness among all but a few evangelical Christians. Christ has become a project to be promoted or a cause to be served instead of a Lord to be obeyed"*[1]

We cannot fake our way or even hide an internal issue as a substitute for this true foundation. If there is an injury that is hindering us from standing upright in the foundation of obedience to Christ, we are going to get caught at some point. One memory that rings true in my mind as a wrestler, one that showed me the importance of a solid foundation, was seeing what happens when the primary foundations of wrestling are forgotten or there is something hindering their proper utilization.

For example, for many wrestlers the first line of defense is the head. But that should not be what they are focused on. The first line of defense for any wrestler should be their stance. If you are not positioned properly in a solid stance, none of the other lines of defense will do any good. If you are standing straight up, you can't use your head to assault another wrestler. If you are bent at the back and leaning too far forward, you have lost all ability to use any of the other defense lines, such as your head, hands, forearms, and hips.

This was never more evident to me than when my team captain, the best wrestler on our team, came out of his stance against the #1 ranked wrestler in the state. He had reached the quarterfinals of the most challenging tournament on our schedule. He knew it was going to be a tough match, but he was confident he could win. He began the match by taking his opponent down with a blast-double leg and riding him out for the entire first period. In the second period, he chose to keep the match on the feet and boom! Another blast-double leg and ride out. The score was 4-0 entering the third period. Now, before I go any further, most wrestlers know that it's usually a good idea to get an easy point by starting from the bottom position and getting an escape. There are reasons this isn't always the case (going against a leg-rider or something of that nature), but it is a typical strategy. However, Eric didn't start on bottom because he was having some back issues stemming from an old baseball injury. He didn't want to feel any pressure on his back, but a 4-0 lead heading into the last period seemed insurmountable, regardless of his ailment.

When the third period started, the other wrestler chose the down position, and this time, unlike the first two periods, he escaped and changed the score to 4-1. With Eric still in control, he took his foot off the gas and was content with pushing his opponent around to waste some time on the clock. The plan seemed to be going fine until Eric's back began complicating the matter. A sharp pain shot into his lower back, and he stood straight up to relieve it. He left his stance for just a second and was planning to go right back to pushing the other wrestler around while waiting for the time to run out. The only issue? His opponent noticed. The other wrestler seized the opportunity as he saw Eric leave the foundation of his stance and went for a desperate throw that squeezed out a win for him. That's exactly how it went down. Eric left his stance for a split second, with less than twenty seconds left in the match, and boom, he was on his back. He lost because he was unable to retain the position that he had learned the first minute, of the first day on the mat.

No matter how much we think we know, no matter how much we think we are remaining in fellowship, if you get out of your stance and no longer follow Jesus, you've lost your foundation. The apostle Paul warned: *"Therefore, let him who thinks he stands take heed that he does not fall"* (1 Corinthians 10:12).

If we don't follow Jesus and gradually become more like Him, we aren't in a proper, secure stance. We can learn all the elements of apologetics in the world, but if our lives don't match Jesus' example, we are simply building knowledge on top of the sand. You may be hanging out with brothers in Christ and having fellowship, but if you are going home and looking at inappropriate stuff on your phone or computer that you would be embarrassed to have Jesus see you looking at, then you are already stumbling and beginning to fall. Apologetics are beneficial, but only if you are walking with, or in a proper stance with, Jesus Christ. So, let's use these tools and take our positions in a solid stance so that when the enemy does attack, we have all of our defenses ready and can use our head, hands, forearms, and hips!

CHAPTER 8

DISCIPLESHIP THROUGH WITNESSING?

> "Have you no wish for others to be saved?
> Then you are not saved yourself. Be sure of that."
> **– Charles Haddon Spurgeon**

THERE WAS a team we would face every year, and their wrestlers boasted remarkable records: 35-1, 40-2, 30-6, while many of our records stood at 26-8 or even 16-10. What accounted for this disparity? We were battle-tested. Our experience came from grappling against genuine competition, whereas this opposing team limited themselves to less challenging, local, dual tournaments. Their aim was to accumulate victories primarily in these tournaments hoping to secure a favorable seed in the qualifying rounds before the post-season. However, this strategy proved vulnerable when individuals who hadn't faced rigorous challenges were thrust into the fierce arena of the post-season.

These individuals found themselves pitted against opponents who had grown accustomed to the meat grinder and made mincemeat of their less experienced opponents. Similarly, in discipleship, the purest comparison to wrestling lies in fulfilling the great commission by sharing the Gospel, during which time one's own deficiencies often remain hidden until confronted with unfamiliar questions. Limiting interactions with like-minded friends only impedes the recognition of one's own blind spots. Gaining confidence does have value, but wrestlers must also comprehend the level of mastery required to achieve victory. Otherwise, they risk being overtaken by better-developed adversaries. This concept was articulated by Paul in his message to the Church in Rome: *"See then the kindness and severity of God: to those who fell, severity, but to you, God's kindness, if you continue in his kindness; for otherwise you, too, will be cut off"* (Romans 11:22).

Paul was free of the blood of all men because he did not shrink back when it came to sharing difficult messages of truth. Regarding evangelism, it is a hard truth for many to realize (i.e., if they are derelict in their duties and are not fully invested in this battle). Sharing the Gospel is the battle test necessary for all believers. It is a surefire way to confirm we are about our Father's business, and in my opinion, it is the quickest way to grow in our walk with Christ! When I first accepted Christ as my personal Lord and Savior, I found myself grappling with a genuine concern: being in fellowship with those who were my age who had grown up within the Church. My own past was tainted by a history of sin, leaving me anxious that my words might unintentionally stray into forbidden territory or that I might inadvertently broach inappropriate subjects. Fearing such mishaps, I took the route of ignorance. I stuck close to my friends who had also recently made a commitment to Christ or even my non-believing companions who accompanied me to church. Yet, as the months went by, a revelation dawned upon me - these newfound companions weren't just acquaintances, they were my spiritual siblings, fellow members of the body of Christ.

Slowly, I engaged in spending more time with them. Then, an opportunity emerged - a proposal from Pastor Joe Schimmel. He asked if I'd be interested in venturing out to Santa Monica's Third St. Promenade to spread the Gospel. To be honest, my initial response was one of reluctance. I felt ill-equipped for such a task and believed I lacked the confidence to articulate and share the Gospel effectively. However, Pastor Joe understood my reservations and reassured me I didn't have to dive headfirst into active evangelistic conversations. Instead, I could simply join the group and observe their interactions, using the experience as a learning opportunity. He probably sensed that if a conversation sparked up I wouldn't be able to suppress the newfound zeal I had for sharing my understanding of Christ. And indeed, he was absolutely right. I still remember when I felt the weight of truth about what the disciples said in the book of Acts: *"...for we cannot stop speaking about what we have seen and heard"* (Acts 4:20).

Though I was there just to listen to the discussions, I couldn't help but speak. I knew Jesus was the truth, and my love for Him did not provide me the ability to "hold my tongue!" I wanted others to know the truth that I had discovered! I attribute that very night as the spiritual microwave of my faith in Christ. By that I mean, after going out and openly sharing my faith I realized I needed to dig into the Word to understand what other people might believe and why. I began to care about people I didn't even know because I realized that I, myself, was once ignorant of the truth. I had been blind to it, but now my eyes were open, and I clearly saw it. Therefore, evangelism has been the chief method of teaching discipleship to the young men and women whom my wife and I work with on a regular basis.

Wrestling and ministry have played out as a synergistic harmony since I came to know Christ as my Savior. If God had me in wrestling, leading young men, then there was no reason not to use it for His glory. In wrestling, you always have those students who develop under your coaching, and you feel like you are the one out there wrestling as they step on the mat and lay it on the line. From my time as an assistant coach and eventually becoming a head coach, this feeling has proven true time and time again. The last disciple I had during my time at Simi Valley High School proved to be one of my most successful, on and off the mat. Nico Hanessian came into wrestling with no previous experience in the sport, but he was willing to listen. He showed a determination to get better, no matter how hard it might be, and I praise the Lord that this has been true in his walk with Christ, as well.

For every great wrestler, there seems to be a match that changes their approach to the game. It has to do with the level of competition, where they beat someone who would have once taken them out. They defeat that opponent, and now the rest of the competition is in trouble. For Nico, this happened at the League Finals during his sophomore year. He defeated someone who had previously taken him down, and I knew he would never lose to him again. I was right, and the next time Nico went up against him, the match wasn't even decided by points because he pinned him in the first period!

I believe this is common in our walks with Christ. From my own vantage point, when it came to Nico's battling for Christ, this match took place on the streets of Ensenada, Mexico, some time at around one in the morning at a lonely taco shop. Who was his opponent? A grizzled taco chef who looked on the outside to be far more stoic than his speech would prove to be. We had already been sharing the Gospel in Mexico, but this time I wanted him to be the one to lead the encounter. I was there by his side to help in any way I could, but he was going to be the one to share the message of Christ. I remember a few minutes before Nico initiated the exchange, he was pacing, getting himself warmed up in prayer, similar to getting warmed up for a match. But this match was different. This wasn't for a perishable crown but for a man's soul. It went very well—so well, in fact, that we have continued to stop by this man's taco shop regularly because we planted a church nearby. We have continued the conversation that Nico started all those years ago, and not only was the encounter fruitful for the one with whom Nico shared, but it was also ultimately extremely fruitful for Nico.

In Paul's letter to Philemon, we read, "... *I pray that the sharing of your faith may become effective for the full knowledge of every good thing that is in us for the sake of Christ*" (Philemon 1:6). The sharing of our faith is also a way for us to remember just how good we have it in Christ! When we share our faith, God brings us to a greater knowledge of every good thing we have in our Savior. This certainly has been the case for me and most definitely is the case for Nico, too!

After this event, I personally saw Nico's walk with Christ get a turbo boost. Not only did he get baptized, but he began sharing the Gospel with everyone he could. He began studying theology more furiously than he did his wrestling tactics. He was so fervent in his desire to share the truth that his entire friend group of brothers and sisters in Christ were lit ablaze with a passion equal to his. It hasn't stopped since that day and has grown even more since that fateful night in Ensenada. As I write this chapter, Nico is finishing his last semester of Bible college in Israel. He also leads our high school and middle school group at our home fellowship with me when he isn't studying abroad.

Nico is one of the better wrestlers in the country, finishing second in a section containing over six hundred teams and far more competitors, which made it the second-biggest tournament in the country. But that pales in comparison to the levels of sanctification and maturation in his walk with Christ. We are now co-laborers for the cause of our Lord Jesus. But this might not have been the case if we had not broken through our anxieties of sharing with those who need to hear the Gospel!

Sharing the Gospel, like wrestling, can never be learned in theory only. It is something that requires practice. You can't merely get better at it by talking with your friends in a holy huddle. You need to get out there and throw yourself into it. It's impossible to determine your areas of weakness and to address them until they've been exposed. This requires us to step out onto the wrestling mat.

Knowing that God has called each believer to this specific service will help us understand that sharing the Gospel isn't only the job of the pastor or ordained clergy member, it is also the job of every blood-bought believer. Second Corinthians chapter 5, verses 18-20 presents it this way:

> *"Now all these things are from God, who reconciled us to Himself through Christ and gave us the ministry of reconciliation, namely, that God was in Christ reconciling the world to Himself, not counting their trespasses against them, and He has committed to us the word of reconciliation. Therefore, we are ambassadors for Christ, as though God were making an appeal through us; we beg you on behalf of Christ, be reconciled to God."*

One might look at the term "ambassador" and see it as a lofty position. Surely this must be made for one who is learned, right? You would at least need to take a class on evangelism, and possibly receive a diploma from a Bible school, right?

Nope.

How about a long-term believer who is a seasoned veteran in their walk?

Nope, again.

Here is the verse which precedes the last quoted passage from Corinthians concerning this calling: *"Therefore, if anyone is in Christ, he is a new creature; the old things passed away; behold, new things have come"* (2 Corinthians 5:17).

So, who is qualified to be ambassador?

It is the "new creature" who is called to be a servant just as Jesus was a servant! If you are in Christ, you are on the varsity team. God has called you, and He is ready to use you! As you grow in your walk, you will learn ways to share. Understand however, that you will never be delivering a cookie-cutter presentation but rather a constant, individualized message, loving those who have yet to come to know Jesus. Make the most of your opportunities and always ask God to make it clear what He wants you to say.

> *"Devote yourselves to prayer, keeping alert in it with an attitude of thanksgiving; praying at the same time for us as well, that God will open up to us a door for the word, so that we may speak forth the mystery of Christ, for which I have also been imprisoned; that I may make it clear in the way I ought to speak. Conduct yourselves with wisdom toward outsiders, making the most of the opportunity. Let your speech always be with grace, as*

though seasoned with salt, so that you will know how you should respond to each person" (Colossians 4:2-6).

We must cry out for the yearning to speak on behalf of Christ and His sacrifice, and for God to strip away our pride! Allow God to show you how He sees the world and how He expresses His love to the lost through the Gospel. The need to share the Gospel may be told in a way that sometimes makes many uncomfortable. However, sometimes it's good to be uncomfortable.

"But the confession had to be made for the sake of others. Do any of you wish to live unto yourselves? If you do, you need saving from selfishness. I have seen it brought as a charge against evangelical religion that we teach men to look to their own salvation first and this is a kind of spiritual selfishness. Ah, but if that salvation means salvation from selfishness, where is the selfishness of it? It is a very material point in salvation to be saved from hardness of heart and carelessness about others. Do you want to go to Heaven alone? I fear you will never go there. **Have you no wish for others to be saved? Then you are not saved yourself. Be sure of that***. What is the most natural plan to use for the salvation of others but to bear your own personal testimony?"*[1] (Emphasis added).

Spurgeon pointed out the fact that Jesus-lovers will want to see others saved, and so did the disciple of the Apostle John,

Polycarp: "*For it is a mark of true and steadfast love for one not only to desire to be saved oneself, but all the brethren also.*"[2]

He continues, "*In terms of our desire to see those saved who are lost, Spurgeon went on to give another punch to the gut we might need, as he pleads with the church to make sure we are doing everything we can: "Oh, my brothers and sisters in Christ, if sinners will be damned, at least let them leap to hell over our bodies; and if they will perish, let them perish with our arms about their knees, imploring them to stay, and not madly to destroy themselves. If hell must be filled, at least let it be filled in the teeth of our exertions and let not one go there unwarned and unprayed for.*"[3]

In Leonard Ravenhill's book, *Why Revival Tarries*, he tells the story of a man named Charlie Peace who was not a peaceful person. Charlie was as wicked as they came and sly as a fox. He was a thief who got away with murder. But Charlie's sowing to the flesh eventually led to his capture and destruction. What Mr. Ravenhill writes about Charlie Peace should convict us as well.

> "*Charlie Peace was a criminal. Laws of God or man curbed him not. Finally, the law caught up with him and he was condemned to death. On the fatal morning in Armley Jail, Leeds, England, he was taken on the death-walk. Before him went the prison chaplain, routinely and sleepily reading some Bible verses. The criminal touched the preacher and asked what he was reading. The Consolation of Religion was the reply. Charlie Peace was shocked at the way the chaplain professionally*

read about hell. Could a man be so unmoved under the very shadow of the scaffold as to lead a fellow human there and yet, dry-eyed, read of a pit that has no bottom into which this fellow must fall? Could this preacher believe the words that there is an eternal fire that never consumes its victims, and yet slide over the phrase without a tremor? Is a man human at all who can say with no tears, 'You will be eternally dying and yet never know the relief that death brings?' All this was too much for Charlie Peace. So, he preached. Listen to his on-the-eve-of-hell sermon. "'Sir,' addressing the preacher, 'if I believed what you and the church of God say that you believe, even if England were covered with broken glass from coast to coast, I would walk over it, if need be, on hands and knees and think it worthwhile living, just to save one soul from an eternal hell like that!'"

"My reader, because the Church has lost Holy Ghost fire, men go to hell-fire! We need a vision of a holy God. God is essentially holy. The cherubim and seraphim were not crying, 'Omnipotent! Omnipotent is the Lord!' not 'Omnipresent! and Omniscient! is the Lord,' but 'Holy! Holy! Holy!' This vast Hebrew concept needs to penetrate our souls again. If I make my bed in hell, if I take the wings of the morning - yet he is there. God compasses us in time; God, the inescapable God, awaits us in eternity. We had better be at peace with him here, and be in the center of His will now!"[4]

Leonard Ravenhill discipled Keith Green, who wrote a song calling out the Church titled, "Asleep in the Light," and I'll close this chapter with a cogent reminder of our need to "get out of bed" and share with those whom God is putting in our path.

"Asleep in the Light"
By Keith Green

Oh, can't you see such sin?
'Cause He brings people to your door
And you turn them away
As you smile and say
"God bless you, be at peace"
And all Heaven just weeps
'Cause Jesus came to your door
You left him out on the streets

Open up, open up
And give yourself away
You see the need, you hear the cries
So how can you delay?
God is calling and you are the one
But like Jonah, you run
He told you to speak but you keep holding it in

Oh, can't you see such sin?
The world is sleeping in the dark
That the church just can't fight
'Cause it's asleep in the light
How can you be so dead
When you've been so well fed?
Jesus rose from the grave
And you, you can't even get out of bed
Oh, Jesus rose from the dead
Come on, get out of your bed

How can you be so numb
Not to care if they come?
You close your eyes and pretend the job is done
You close your eyes and pretend the job is done
Don't close your eyes, don't pretend the job is done

CHAPTER 9
KNOWING YOUR ENEMY IN THE CONTEXT OF DISCIPLESHIP

"This is the true athlete - he who, in the great stadium, the fair world, is crowned for the true victory over all the passions. For He who prescribes the contest is the Almighty God, and he who awards the prize is the only begotten Son of God. Angels and gods are spectators; and the contest, embracing all the varied exercises, is *"not against flesh and blood,"* (Ephesians 6:12) but against the spiritual powers of inordinate passions that work through the flesh. He who obtains the mastery in these struggles, and overthrows the tempter, menacing, as it were, with certain contests, wins immortality. For the sentence of God in most righteous judgment is infallible. The spectators are summoned to the contest, and the athletes contend in the stadium; the one, who has obeyed the directions of the trainer wins the day.

For to all, all rewards proposed by God are equal; and he himself is unimpeachable. And he who has power receives mercy, and he that has exercised will is mighty."
– **Clement of Alexandria**

As a young wrestler, my life was filled with adrenaline, competition, and a strong sense of invincibility. I was, however, lost, living a reckless life without any belief in Christ and thus no moral compass. My nights were consumed by drinking, and I often found myself in the middle of multiple fights. Church was a distant thought, and I only visited once or twice throughout my high school years. Though I grew up in a conservative home, my actions and beliefs denied him. However, amidst my chaotic lifestyle, I found an unexpected fascination with a team that was not my own—the Calvary Chapel Church Boyz.

Their unique singlets and a website dedicated to their wrestlers made me greatly admire them. I would watch them at tournaments, longing to warm up like them, wear the same shoes, and wrestle with the same passion they displayed. The Church Boyz had a section on their website where each wrestler shared their favorite Scripture verse. Bryan Osuna, who was a multi-time state placer, had posted a passage that captured my attention and would stay with me forever.

Osuna's favorite verse was Ephesians 6:12, which states: *"For we do not wrestle against flesh and blood, but against principalities, against powers, against the rulers of the darkness of this age, against spiritual hosts of wickedness in the heavenly places."*

I didn't fully understand the meaning of the verse, but the fact wrestling was mentioned in the Bible intrigued me. It sparked my curiosity and stuck in my mind, even though I continued to live a life that contradicted its meaning and eventually turned to atheism. The turning point came one fateful night when I gave my life to Christ. As I returned home after that life-changing decision, I couldn't shake off the memory of Bryan's favorite verse. I immediately sat at my computer and looked up "wrestling in the Bible."

I was astonished to find the story of Jacob wrestling with God in the thirty-second chapter of Genesis and how that encounter earned him the name "Israel." But what struck me the most was the verse Bryan had shared—Ephesians 6:12. Little did I know then, but this verse would shape my journey with Christ and become the first verse of the Bible I ever memorized.

From that day forward, my life began to change. My aimless, reckless habits were replaced with a newfound purpose and direction. I started attending church regularly and was surrounded by people who genuinely loved and followed Jesus. Their faith and support guided me along the path of redemption. As I pursued my passion for wrestling, I not only wrestled on the mat but also in battles in the spiritual realm. I learned to lean on Christ's strength, seeking victory from the sport I loved and in my spiritual walk. My focus shifted from earthly achievements to eternal rewards.

In time, I understood the verse that had captured my attention years before. Wrestling wasn't just a physical competition;

it was an analogy for our daily spiritual struggles. Armed with this newfound understanding, I wrestled with my doubts, fears, and sins, leaning on God's Word and His grace.

This verse found in Paul's letter to the church of Ephesus is the main focal point for us in this chapter. It helps us realize we are in a spiritual battle, and it reminds us of the actual battle which we are so apt to forget. In fact, when Paul wrote to the Corinthians, he was dealing with a grievous sin issue in the church and, as a follow-up, he warned the Church to remember his heart toward the repentant one who had sinned. But how he warned them brings us to an important point.

Paul mentioned that when they were not accepting of a brother who repented and came back to the church, they were "not ignorant of his [Satan's] schemes" (2 Corinthians 2:11b). The goal of this chapter is to help us recognize our enemy's tactics and see how the Church throughout history has wrestled with the aspect of "knowing your enemy" in the context of discipleship.

Every wrestler can vividly recall their most difficult match. They can probably still picture their opponent, where they stood in the bracket and the amount of research they did about their opponent. For me, my toughest match came at a time when I least expected it. During my junior year, I was ranked very high heading into CIF, and I believed I would have an easy first match. I looked up my opponent's name but didn't know much about him. His school was in the same league as a formidable team in our section, Temecula Valley. I assumed he didn't win his league, and I would have a smooth first-round match. But that wasn't the case at all. I got trounced. I was overmatched, outgunned, and simply not strong enough. Within the first thirty seconds I was out on blood time, something I had never experienced before in a match. I was down 2-0, and my expectations for an easy victory were shattered. Little did I know, the guy I was facing had been busy with football and had criteria which gave him a higher ranking prior to the tournament. He ended up beating me and eventually placing in the state tournament, making me realize that what I thought was a warmup match was instead a formidable challenge. I'm not sure if I would have beaten him, but knowing my opponent better could have helped me wrestle more effectively.

Similarly, in our walk with Christ, we must know our opponent if we want to win the battles of this spiritual war. God makes it clear in the Scriptures how the enemy will attack, which allows us to fully prepare ourselves for skirmishes. There are three formidable foes described in the Bible who wage war against us: the world, the flesh, and the Devil.

The world makes things difficult for us. According to the Parable of the Sower, there is a type of soil that doesn't allow the seed of God's Word to take deep root. It is choked by the thorns of worldly anxiety and the deceitfulness of wealth (Matthew 13:7; 13:22). When it comes to the flesh, both the world and Satan attack weaknesses that remain and either choke out or remove the word immediately after it is sown. We must be diligent to make our calling and election sure by resisting the devil and drawing near to God. Satan, the adversary, "prowls around like a roaring lion, seeking someone to devour" (1 Peter

5:8). He employs various tactics to deceive and tempt us away from a relationship with God. To understand the importance of knowing our enemy, we can learn from all-pro safety John Lynch's experience against the Oakland Raiders during Super Bowl XXXVII in 2003.

When Lynch was mic'd up for the game, he can be heard calling out what the play was going to be right before it happened. He told the eventual Super Bowl MVP, Dexter Jackson, that the play was going to be a "Sluggo Seam," and Jackson stepped in front of the pass and intercepted the ball. He would later do the same thing and take it all the way to cap off a Tampa Bay Buccaneers blowout victory over the Oakland Raiders 48-21. In the mic'd up highlight of the game, Lynch can be heard talking to his teammates on the sidelines and in the huddle saying: "They're too predictable. We know them."

"Monty, on that last one he checked. Remember how Gruden was telling us they call two plays? That's what he did."

"Mike, every play they've run, we ran in practice. It's unreal."

But the interesting part of this backstory is that the Buccaneers' coach that year was John Gruden.

The year before, Gruden was coaching the same Oakland Raiders that the Buccaneers were playing against. But the Raiders decided to trade John Gruden to the Tampa Bay Buccaneers, only to face the very coach that built them into a championship-quality team. Imagine if John Lynch had decided he didn't care about the enemy's tactics and simply wanted to react when they came to him. Not only would he have likely lost his job, but what coach could trust him enough to put him into the game? When our Coach has done the hard work of laying out the game plan because He knows the enemy's game plan and has handed it over to us, we'd better do our best to study what He has given to us. This action was abundantly clear to the Early Church and should, therefore, be abundantly clear to us.

Clement of Jerusalem wrote the "Catechetical Lecture," which instructed newly baptized Christians about what the Christian life would look like after baptism. He warned believers about the different aspects of Satan and his attacks. At the onset of the last five chapters of his lectures to the newly baptized believers, he begins with this Scripture verse: *"Be sober, be vigilant; because your adversary the devil walks about like a roaring lion, seeking whom he may devour"* (1 Peter 5:8).

Clement recognized that the first thing a Christian needs to understand is that we are engaged in a spiritual war, and we need to be on our guard. Getting drunk and getting yourself outside of your right mind will leave an opening for the "darts of the Devil." In the service of Baptism, one renounces the works of Satan and turns to Christ's victory as our own. We are called to renounce sin and avoid indulging in the Devil's temptations. We should be sober and vigilant, aware of the Devil's schemes (2 Corinthians 2:11). By turning to Christ and renouncing Satan, we are freed from the bondage of sin and welcomed into the kingdom of God. However, we must remain watchful and guarded, for the adversary, the Devil, seeks to devour us. Clement finished his 19th lecture with the following three stanzas:

"When therefore you renounce Satan, utterly breaking all your covenant with him, that ancient *league with hell* Isaiah 28:15, there is opened to you the paradise of God, which He planted towards the East, whence for his transgression our first father was banished; and a symbol of this was your turning from West to East, the place of light. Then you were told to say, 'I believe in the Father, and in the Son, and in the Holy Ghost, and in one Baptism of repentance. ' Of which things we spoke to you at length in the former Lectures, as God's grace allowed us.

Guarded therefore by these discourses, *be sober*. For our adversary the devil, as was just now read, as a roaring lion, walks about, seeking whom he may devour (1 Peter 5:8). But though in former times death was mighty and devoured, at the holy Laver of regeneration God has wiped away every tear from off all faces. For you shall no more mourn, now that you have put off the old man; but you shall keep holy day, *clothed in the garment of salvation* (Isaiah 61:10), even Jesus Christ.

And these things were done in the outer chamber. But if God will, when in the succeeding lectures on the Mysteries we have entered into the Holy of Holies, we shall there know the symbolic meaning of the things which are there performed. Now to God the Father, with the Son and the Holy Ghost, be glory, and power, and majesty, forever and ever. Amen."[1]

CHAPTER 10
THE TOUGHEST BATTLE FOR A DISCIPLE

"Pornography is *all* anticipation and *no* satisfaction. It provides exaggerated levels of excitement, which no real woman could ever provide."
– Tim Barnett

THE PREVIOUS CHAPTER laid out the importance of understanding we are in a spiritual war, but this chapter will go on to specifically address the toughest battle for most men (and a growing number of women) and present a strategy to pin down this seemingly insurmountable opponent. While we may like to forget our worst losses, they can burrow down into a place in the mind that frequently reminds us how we fell short. When these moments arise, we must remember, "There is therefore now no condemnation in Christ Jesus."

Conviction, yes.

Condemnation, no.

It is also important to bear in mind the victories that come to us during extremely limited odds. For me, the victory I will never forget is one over someone who was nicknamed the "Crushin' Russian." My league's final opponent was 40-1 going into our match and stood around six and a half feet to my five-foot-seven frame. I was not even expected to get into the finals. My ranking heading into the tournament was going to force me to get a number of upsets in order to punch my ticket into the finals to face the one who was expected to stand atop the podium. It seemed like an insurmountable task just to make it through the entire six minutes required, let alone beat the "Crushin' Russian." But if I wanted to secure a league championship my junior year, I'd have to do this, and the weight of the challenge ahead was immense. Doubt crept into my mind, threatening to shatter my confidence before I even stepped onto the wrestling mat. But there was one moment I truly believe played a pivotal role in securing an unlikely victory in a match I wasn't expected to prevail.

My favorite wrestler was one of my closest friends, Kevin, and he was one of the best wrestlers in the entire nation. Kevin was not only a fellow team captain but also the wrestler I looked up to the most. His prowess on the mat was awe-inspiring, and I would hang onto every word of wrestling advice he had to offer. Beyond his technical guidance, he was an unwavering source of support, going above and beyond to help me reach the next level. His dad would drive me to off-season tournaments and take me to practices outside our own, selflessly investing time and effort in my growth as a wrestler. This may sound sentimental, but the confidence Kevin had in me to take out this formidable opponent, the "Crushin' Russian," was precisely what I needed to enter the arena that day with a glimmer of hope. His unwavering belief in my capabilities planted a seed of determination within me, pushing me beyond my known limits. Not only did I get the first takedown, but I was able to wrestle a much smarter match than he did and walk out of there with a thrilling 4-3 win. And I secured a league title that nobody saw coming.

I realized not long after that moment that having someone you deeply respect come alongside you—someone who has walked the path of defeating tough opponents and witnessing their unwavering confidence in your ability to achieve victory—can create for you an immeasurable advantage. Of course, the ultimate challenge was mine alone, and I had to summon every ounce of determination and skill to meet it. But knowing that someone had my back and believed in me meant the world to me and made a huge difference. That day on the wrestling mat, I saw how when someone else believes in you, you can ignite a fire within your soul that propels you beyond your own accepted limits, inspiring you to achieve greatness against all odds.

WHO OR WHAT IS GOING TO BE YOUR TOUGHEST BATTLE?

Your toughest battle will most likely be one that has taken men captive far more than many would like to admit. It is one that has taken down kings, prophets, and men of great wisdom. In fact, when Paul gives the fruits of the flesh in Galatians chapter 5, the first three aspects of the flesh deal directly with this sin: Sexual Immorality, Impurity, and Sensuality.

I'm sure for most people reading this, they would admit the toughest battle for many is pornography. In Paul's second letter to Timothy, we read some of the human characteristics that will be seen during the end times. One of the warnings in this list of end times vices comes in the form of men becoming "lovers of pleasure, rather than lovers of God" (2 Timothy 3:4). But what precedes these words is the statement that men will be "lovers of self" (2 Timothy 3:2). You see, in this selfish day and age, men have become so enamored with their own pleasures that, for many, the love of others has gone by the wayside.

In the very next verse, we see the love of the family will also be lost. In Second Timothy chapter 3, verse 3, we are given a specific Greek word to describe the lack of love that will happen in the end times. The word used in this verse is ἄστοργοι or astorgoi—a word combination similar to A-theist. The prefix "A" means "without," and "storgoi" means "family love." There will be a lack of family love prevalent in the end times. Because so many men (and women) have become lovers of self and pleasure, they have lacked the love of their own family that would typically hinder them from looking at sinful material and thus bring to ruin the marriage that God has blessed. Because so many have grown accustomed to appeasing their own palate and do not care about grieving the Holy Spirit, men have become lovers of pleasure rather than lovers of God. To love

God is to know Him and wish to obey Him. In John 14:15, Jesus says, "If you love me, keep my commandments."

1 John 1:5-6 says this: *"This is the message we have heard from Him and announce to you, that God is Light, and in him there is no darkness at all. If we say that we have fellowship with him and yet walk in the darkness, we lie and do not practice the truth."* And in 1 John 3:7-10, we are even given the guidelines by which we identify God's children:

> *"Little children, make sure no one deceives you; the one who practices righteousness is righteous, just as he is righteous; the one who practices sin is of the devil; for the devil has sinned from the beginning. The Son of God appeared for this purpose, to destroy the works of the devil. No one who is born of God practices sin, because his seed abides in him; and he cannot sin, because he is born of God. By this the children of God and the children of the devil are obvious: anyone who does not practice righteousness is not of God, nor the one who does not love his brother."*

When we place our own pleasures above the obedience that God requires of us, we forget the great sacrifice Jesus made in open shame on our behalf. This chain of self-love is the Devil's trifecta that will bring many would-be, God-glorifying families to ruin. Fathers have allowed God to take a back seat to their own pleasure, to their own self, and to cast aside the family love that would motivate them to repent of such sin. Because their needs are placed above those of the family, the marriage and the family's fate is in calamity. But it is also pertinent to point out that man is not saved by good works. "We are saved by grace through faith" (Ephesians 2:8-9), yet having said this, there is fruit that is going to be evident in a believer's life that will mark them as an obvious child of God (Matthew 7:15-20; 1 John 3:10).

I do not want anyone to think that because they have stumbled in this area that it means they do not know the Lord. Scripture tells us, *"My little children, I am writing these things to you so that you may not sin. And if anyone sins, we have an Advocate with the Father, Jesus Christ the righteous"* (1 John 2:1). These warnings are being written for the same purpose—that we may not sin against God in this area of our lives. God commands us to be obedient to His calling and to test ourselves to see if we are in the faith (2 Corinthians 13:5). I encourage anyone who knowingly continues to sin to take account today (Hebrews 10:26), and not to wait for tomorrow. Do not dance on the fence. Confess your sins! For if you do, *"He is faithful and righteous to forgive us our sins and to cleanse us from all unrighteousness"* (1 John 1:9).

The Christian walk is to be one of victory and not defeat. In Paul's letter to the Romans, we are told that those in Christ Jesus are "more than conquerors" (Romans 8:37). Not by their own strength, but by the power of Jesus Christ and the Holy Spirit! For apart from Him we can do nothing (John 15:5).

Various warnings come to mind when we think about what Jesus told His disciples regarding this subject. When Christ brought the audience's thoughts captive to the idea that we need to keep a "kingdom perspective" in Matthew 6, He contrasted men fasting for man's approval versus fasting for God's approval. He then warned that we should not store up our treasures on Earth because these things are fleeting and inconsequential regarding our ultimate, eternal dwelling place. He then said these words: *"The eye is the lamp of the body; so then if your eye is clear, your whole body will be full of light. But if your eye is bad, your whole body will be full of darkness. If then the light that is in you is darkness, how great is the darkness"* (Matthew 6:22-23).

These words reveal that man's heart needs to be fully devoted to God and not his own possessions. We should also focus our attention on glorifying God. If we use the eyes God gave us to stare upon things that He sees as wicked, we will be encompassed by darkness. Jesus' warning can also be summed up in His answer when asked about the greatest commandment. He told us the greatest commandment was to *"love the Lord your God with all of your heart, and with all of your soul, and with all of your mind...the second is like it, to love your neighbor as yourself"* (Matthew 22:37-39).

Many of the men who are being entertained by pornographic material would not want their wives to be watching pornography. I am also certain that they would not want their daughter to be seen on film sleeping with men. If we truly love God and wish to obey Him, we shouldn't see people as objects. We must recognize that the love of the Father transcends all others and is not a love that is common or ordinary. But that type of love doesn't make sense to a lost world. If we fill our hearts with the love of God, it will bring about a reverential fear, and we will not want to dishonor our beloved King. If we love God with all our minds and place the helmet of salvation on our heads, we will not allow wicked thoughts to enter, and we will correct ourselves so that we will not have to be disciplined. If we use all the strength God has given us to battle against temptation, He will give us the strength to endure it (1 Corinthians 10:13).

Any conversation about pornography in light of Scripture should start and end with Jesus' warning in Matthew 5:27-30. In this passage, and much of the chapter, Jesus makes it clear that He is after our hearts. He is not after mere outward religion. He doesn't want us to draw near with our lips but be far from Him with our hearts. He is not after those who wish to do wickedness in their heart, even though they do not do it out in the open. The condition of our hearts is clearly paramount to Jesus. He warns us of the perils that come from having hatred in our hearts and then states this: *"You have heard that it was said, YOU SHALL NOT COMMIT ADULTERY; but I say to you that everyone who looks at a woman with lust for her has already committed adultery with her in his heart"* (Matthew 5:27-28, emphasis added).

And lest we think that pornography cannot become a salvation issue, here is what Jesus has to say: *"If your right eye makes you stumble, tear it out and throw it from you; for it is better for you to lose one of the parts of your body, than for your whole body to be thrown into hell. If your right hand makes you stumble, cut it off and throw it from you; for it is better for you to lose one of the parts of your body, than for your whole body to go into hell"* (Matthew 5:29-30).

For some people, plucking out an eye and cutting off an arm could be symbolic of turning off the computer. If one cannot use a computer without longing for something that is aiming to damn the soul, throw it out. Better to be computerless in this world than be joyless in eternity. There are certain precautions that we may need to take to keep this evil from taking over our hearts. There is a love for God that should also bring out a reverential respect and fear of Him.

This is not a mere fight—this is war! We need to recognize the spiritual warfare that is going on. One of the chief dangers men face when fighting against sin is not knowing who the enemy is. But the Bible gives us exact instructions on sin, who the enemy is, and how to defeat them. The Bible says we aren't fighting merely against flesh and blood. It is not only our fleshly desires that tempt us, but a cunning enemy who brings temptation into our lives. The battle is not only won on our knees but with our comrades.

We have fellow soldiers in the army of God who need to come together and fight this battle with us. In Exodus chapter 17, we read about the battle between Amalek and Israel. Not only did Moses raise his arms to Heaven, but his brothers came to his aid when he didn't have the strength to hold them up himself: *"So, it came about when Moses held his hand up, that Israel prevailed, and when he let his hand down, Amalek prevailed. But Moses' hands were heavy. Then they took a stone and put it under him, and he sat on it; and Aaron and Hur supported his hands, one on one side and one on the other. Thus, his hands were steady until the sun set. So, Joshua overwhelmed Amalek and his people with the edge of the sword"* (Exodus 17:11-13).

This is where the Body of Christ needs to step in and step up. We need to hold our brother's arms up when they lack the strength to keep going. We need to make sure we hold each other accountable. If someone is struggling with sin, they need to find a brother they can confide in and ask for a prayer covering. James chapter 5, verse 16 puts it this way: *"Therefore, confess your sins to one another, and pray for one another so that you may be healed. The effective prayer of the righteous man can accomplish much."*

Don't let your search engine know more about your struggles than a brother in the Lord. Pray without ceasing. Do not simply pray God will get you through the struggle; pray until God brings you through the struggle. Lean on your brothers so you can carry one another's burdens and fulfill the law of Christ (Galatians 6:1-2). Find your "Kevin" who can encourage you when you are in the battle. Find someone who has had victory and learn how they did it. Then, attain victory yourself and share that with those who may be struggling!

CHAPTER 11
FINISHING THE RACE SET BEFORE US BY JOE SCHIMMEL

"This able wrestler [the apostle Paul], therefore, exhorts us to the struggle for immortality, that we may be crowned [1 Cor. 9:24-27], and may deem the crown precious, namely, that which is acquired by our struggle, but which does not encircle us of its own accord."
– Irenaeus

I COUNT it a blessing to be invited to write a chapter for a book on discipleship for a brother whom I have had the privilege of discipling. Chad has not only proven to be a great disciple of the Lord Jesus Christ, but he's also a great husband to my eldest daughter, Holly, and a diligent father to four of my precious grandchildren. Early in my ministry, a good brother who had joined our fellowship said he had observed that our fellowship was producing what he called "strong converts." Of course, any success we have had through the years is all the result of the Lord's grace and the work of His Spirit and Word among us. We count Chad as one of those prized disciples who is making other strong disciples (2 Timothy 2:2). It is critical when making disciples we constantly point those we are discipling to Jesus, for God's ultimate objective is that we are "conformed to the image of His Son, so that He would be the firstborn among many brethren" (Romans 8:29b).

Another reason I am blessed to contribute a chapter to Chad's book on wrestling with discipleship is it almost didn't happen. In 2020, I found out that I had AFib (Atrial Fibrillation), and my heart, unbeknownst to me, had been racing about one hundred and fifty beats per minute for nearly six months. An echocardiogram revealed my heart had been weakened to only a thirty-four percent ejection fraction. I saw a renowned cardiologist in Santa Barbara, who strongly warned me not to get COVID. He told me in the presence of my wife, "Joe, your heart is incredibly weak right now. Don't get Covid. *You won't survive!*"

Just a week after receiving this warning, sure enough, I got COVID!

I wasn't sure just how weak my heart could actually get before it finally gave out, but the echocardiogram technician's words were not very reassuring. I wrestled earnestly with the Lord in prayer, "Lord, while I would love to go to be with You I have so much more I want to do for You before I leave Earth. Is this it? Will I not see my wife, children, grandchildren, my extended family or my brothers and sisters in Christ in this life again?" I reminded Him of what He, of course, already knew, that I was in the middle of producing what I believed was a life-impacting documentary I thought He had laid upon my heart. I knew, however, that in His infinite knowledge and His perfect will, He might have a totally different plan, of which I wasn't aware! I knew I had to trust the Lord for whatever the outcome.

I continued to seek Him earnestly in prayer and quote encouraging scriptures like, "To live is Christ, and to die is gain," (Philippians 1:21), and "My flesh and my heart may fail, but God is the strength of my heart and my portion forever" (Psalm 73:26). Suddenly the Lord began to graciously speak to my heart. "You will survive!" It was not audible, but it was clearly discernible.

After five days in the hospital, they discharged me just in time to celebrate Christmas with my family. A doctor told my wife and me, "Joe, it would have been a miracle if your heart improved at all in that condition, but for it to become normal and return to full strength overnight is an incredible miracle!" We just thank God for every victory He graciously gives us.

As we can see from the quote of the Early Church Father, Irenaeus, at the beginning of this chapter, the early Christians understood that believers were in a wrestling match against the foe of their eternal souls. Though Jesus had won the victory through His death for our sins on the Cross and His glorious resurrection, only those who stand firm in the faith in Christ emerge victorious on the last day. *"Now I make known to you, brethren, the Gospel which I preached to you, which also you received, in which also you stand, by which also you are saved, if you hold fast the word which I preached to you, unless you believed in vain"* (1 Corinthians 15:1-2).

When it comes to discipleship, it's critical that we do our best to present those under our love and care as complete in Christ as possible. The best way to do this is to diligently teach the Holy Scripture (2 Timothy 4:2-4) and to faithfully proclaim Jesus as Lord. The goal of wise pastoral ministry is to proclaim Jesus and exhort those we are discipling with all wisdom so that we may present them perfect or mature before Christ on that final day. The apostle Paul gives the following instruction to the church at Colossae in a passage that has been an ever-present guide to me in my pastoral ministry:

> *"And although you were formerly alienated and hostile in mind, engaged in evil deeds, yet he has now reconciled you in His fleshly body through death, in order to present you before Him holy and blameless and beyond reproach—if indeed you continue in the faith firmly established and steadfast, and not moved away from the hope of the gospel…*
>
> *…We proclaim Him, admonishing every man and teaching every man with all wisdom, so that we may present every man complete in Christ"* (Colossians 1:21-23a, 28).

This means we are to equip believers to be prepared for trials and tribulations so that they may stand and persevere through hard times. Indeed, Luke summed up much of Paul and Silas's ministry to the Church by declaring they were "'strengthening the souls of the disciples, encouraging them to continue in the faith,' and saying, 'Through many tribulations we must enter the kingdom of God'" (Acts 14:22).

I learned several valuable lessons through the fiery trial that almost took my life during the height of COVID. One was the importance of keeping in good shape. God made me naturally strong, and I never really felt a pressing need to consistently work out. But as I age, I've learned it's important to take proper care of the temple He has entrusted to me so that I might better serve Him. However - and this is the crazy thing - as important as it is to be disciplined with regards to eating properly and exercising regularly, it is far more important for us to feed and exercise ourselves spiritually if we are to be effective disciples: "*[D]iscipline yourself for the purpose of godliness; for bodily discipline is only of little profit, but godliness is profitable for all things, since it holds promise for the present life and also for the life to come*" (1 Timothy 4:7b-8).

The root word of discipline is disciple. If a disciple is to grow in Christ, he must discipline himself unto godliness. The Greek word Paul uses for discipline is "gumnazo," from which we get the English word "gymnasium." Paul used the imagery of the day, when the Grecian Olympics were quite popular, to inspire Christians to be athletes for Christ. But millions of professing Christians, like Peter Pan, refuse to grow up and seek maturation. The "Peter Pan Syndrome" is not cute to God - it's reprehensible. Many Christians grieve the Spirit and break God's heart when they are content to be binky, baba babies, soiled in their diapers and failing to go on to maturity. This was prophesied by the apostle Paul, who solemnly warned Timothy to preach the Word in light of the coming apostasy, wherein many will prefer spiritual junk food to the pure milk and meat of God's Word (2 Timothy 4:1-4). Paul stated he was blameless when it came to his accountability before the Lord with regard to the souls or the blood of others because he was faithful to preach the whole counsel of God and did not compromise in his proclamation of God's Word.

> *"Therefore, I testify to you this day that I am innocent of the blood of all men. For I did not shrink back from declaring to you the whole will of God"* – Acts 20:26-27.

When I was invited to preach in the Netherlands, I was told that doctors who failed to prescribe proper medicine were called "Stinky Doctors." This is because their patients languished in festering sores and with deadly diseases, often being given nothing more than Band-Aids. When a doctor prescribes the wrong medicine, it is considered malpractice and can prove fatal. How many Christian leaders are guilty of spiritual malpractice because they want to be popular or don't want to offend someone? God has not called us to a life of ease but to holiness. May the Lord help us faithfully preach the Word so we may bear much fruit to His eternal glory! After Paul declared that we are to discipline ourselves for godliness because it holds promises not only for this life but for the eternal life to come, he used another familiar athletic term when he stated: *"For it is for this we labor and **strive**, because we have fixed our hope on the* *living God, who is the Savior of all men, especially of believers"* (1 Timothy 4:10: Emphasis added).

The Greek word for strive is from the word "agōn," from which we get the English word agonize. Jesus used the present tense, imperative form of this word when He warned the lost to enter the narrow gate that leads to eternal life.

> *"Strive* [Gk. Agōnizesthe] *to enter through the narrow gate, for many, I say to you, will seek to enter and will not be able"* (Luke 13:24).
>
> *"Fight* (agōnizou) *the good fight* (agōna) *of faith; take hold of the eternal life to which you were called, and you made the good confession in the presence of many witnesses"* (1 Timothy 6:12).

Paul had already warned Timothy at the beginning of the chapter, *"But the Spirit explicitly says that in later times some will fall away from the faith, paying attention to deceitful spirits and doctrines of demons"* (1 Timothy 4:1). He warned Timothy in chapter 1 to fight the good fight and hold on to his faith, so that his faith would not become shipwrecked as it had for others who fell into apostasy.

> *"This command I entrust to you, Timothy, my son, in accordance with the prophecies previously made concerning you, that by them you fight the good fight, keeping faith and a good conscience, which some have rejected and suffered shipwreck in regard to their faith. Among these are Hymenaeus and Alexan-*

der, whom I have handed over to Satan, so that they will be taught not to blaspheme" (1 Timothy 1:18-20).

If Timothy is to withstand the temptation of the world, the flesh, and the Devil, he must fight the good fight and hold fast to eternal life. Paul reminds Timothy that Christians are spiritual athletes and they have a race to run and win. In Second Timothy, chapter 2, verse 5, Paul warns, *"And if someone likewise competes as an athlete, he is not crowned as a victor unless he competes according to the rules."*

In the Greco-Roman world, the Grecian Olympic participants had to swear an oath before a statue of Zeus. If an athlete was found to have broken the rules or cheated during a competition, he would automatically be disqualified. The guidelines we are given to enter the race are to simply forsake the broad road that leads to destruction and to get on the track that is described by Jesus as the narrow road that leads to life (Matthew 7:13-14). The broad road leads to hell, while the narrow road leads to eternal life in the heavenly kingdom. This is why would-be disciples are warned that they must repent (Luke 13:5).

The beautiful Greek word translated as "repentance" most often in the New Testament is "metanoia." Metanoia means to have a change of heart and will, which leads to a change in direction and behavior. Repentance is like a spiritual U-turn whereby we get off the broad road that leads to destruction and get on the narrow road that leads to life. Jesus instructs would-be participants in the Christian race that if they wish to be His disciples, then they must begin the race in the following way:

> *"And He was saying to them all, "If anyone wishes to come after Me, he must deny himself, and take up his cross daily and follow Me. For whoever wishes to save his life will lose it, but whoever loses his life for My sake, he is the one who will save it. For what is a man profited if he gains the whole world, and loses or forfeits himself? For whoever is ashamed of Me and My words, the Son of Man will be ashamed of him when He comes in His glory, and the glory of the Father and of the holy angels"* (Luke 9:23-26).

If we are to finish the race set before us, we first need to make sure we get on the right track. But that can only take place when we take up our cross, deny ourselves, and follow Jesus.

For Paul, the race of salvation set before us is not a mere sprint that ends at an altar but a journey that begins with salvation and isn't over until we die and go to be with the Lord (or at our Lord's glorious return). But in the ancient Olympic games, athletes were given strict instructions and had to train strictly for a minimum of ten months before the event. If they were caught cheating, they were disgraced and stripped of their crowns. Even in modern times Olympic athletes have been disqualified or stripped of their medals. From October 1968 to December 2022, the International Olympic Committee (IOC) has stripped 154 medals from Olympic athletes. The Christian athlete doesn't win his race by simply going up to an altar call, but by persevering in his faith until the end. The Christian athlete must keep his eyes on Jesus and heed his warnings as he presses on to the prize.

"I am coming quickly; hold fast what you have, so that no one will take your crown" – Revelation 3:11. Jesus warned His apostles that only those who endure to the end would be saved. *"You will be hated by all because of My name, but it is the one who has endured to the end who will be saved…*

… Do not fear those who kill the body but are unable to kill the soul; but rather fear Him who is able to destroy both soul and body in hell…

…Therefore everyone who confesses Me before men, I will also confess him before My Father who is in heaven. But whoever denies Me before men, I will also deny him before My Father who is in heaven" (Matthew 10:22, 28, 32-33).

For James, the race is an obstacle course full of trials, but one that promises the crown of life to those who persevere to the end. After Jesus' death, James contrasted the crown of life with spiritual death (James 1:12-16).

In Paul's mind, the race set before us is both a marathon and an obstacle course. The runner must not only run with endurance, but also wrestle against the powers of darkness (Ephesians 6:12). He must box, beating down the ungodly, evil cravings of his old man. *"Therefore, I run in such a way, as not without aim; I box in such a way, as not beating the air; but I discipline my body and make it my slave, so that, after I have preached to others, I myself will not be disqualified"* (1 Corinthians 9:26-27).

Yet Paul's warning is that just as the Olympian must stay the course, so must the believer finish his race if he is not to be disqualified and to be finally crowned. Paul warned the Corinthians they were not to be deceived into believing the lie that they could live in wicked rebellion against God and still inherit the kingdom of God. *"Or do you not know that the unrighteous will not inherit the Kingdom of God? Do not be deceived; neither fornicators, nor idolaters, nor adulterers, nor effeminate, nor homosexuals, nor thieves, nor the covetous, nor drunkards, nor revilers, nor swindlers, will inherit the Kingdom of God"* (1 Corinthians 6:9-10).

In his book, *Word Pictures in the New Testament*, the late great A. T. Robertson, who is heralded as the "prince of Greek scholars," when commenting on Paul beating his body down lest he be disqualified, he stated, "Most writers take Paul to refer to the possibility of his rejection in his personal salvation at the end of the race. It is a humbling thought for us all to see this wholesome fear instead of smug complacency in this greatest of all heralds of Christ."[1]

Lest we are tempted to downplay the seriousness of Paul's solemn warning that we need to finish the Christian race, Paul would later employ the same Greek adjective (adokimos) in his warning to the Corinthians. He warns that some have still refused to repent of their rebellion against God and that they need to seriously examine themselves to establish whether or not they are truly in the faith and indwelt by the Lord Jesus Christ (2 Corinthians 12:21; 13:5).

It is noteworthy that those whom Paul declares will fail the test or be disqualified (adokimos) are not those who struggle with sin and still continue in the faith, but rather those who continue to practice sin and refuse to repent, (e.g., those who have "***not repented** of the impurity, immorality, and sensuality which they have practiced*") (2 Corinthians 12:21: Emphasis added). There is a huge difference between those who stumble on the racetrack of faith into the mud and get back up and those who altogether abandon the straight and narrow road and choose to wallow in the mud with the pigs. All of us will stumble on the racetrack of faith from time to time and sometimes badly; however, if we get back up and confess our sins and stay the course, He is faithful to forgive us and cleanse us from all unrighteousness (1 John 1:7-9).

The race of faith has a beginning, a middle, and an end. Through the New Testament writers, God revealed that there are three phases of time relative to being saved. These includes the past, when we're born again or regenerated by grace through faith (Ephesians 2:8-9); the present, as we are walking the road to salvation with Jesus and "being saved" (σωζεσθε) (1 Corinthians 1:18, 15:2); and final salvation when we are said to be saved in the future tense at the day of the Lord (Matthew 10:22; 24:13; Romans 5:9; 13:11; 1 Thessalonians 5:9-10; Hebrews 9:28). Our salvation race begins when we respond to Jesus' call and are born again. It continues as we are sanctified through faith in Jesus and the ongoing work of the Holy Spirit and the Word of God. It's completed when we die in faith and are glorified with resurrected bodies at the Lord's Second Advent.

Paul goes on to encourage the Corinthian Christians by declaring the Lord is faithful to provide the strength they need to run their race victoriously. *"No temptation has overtaken you, but such as is common to man; and God is faithful, who will not allow you to be tempted beyond what you are able, but with the temptation will provide the way of escape also, so that you will be able to endure it. Therefore, my beloved, flee from idolatry"* (1 Corinthians 10:13-14).

Paul also used the racetrack imagery when he wrote to the Philippians, declaring that he was pressing on in the race of faith so that he could be included in the resurrection of the dead. For Paul, the resurrection that he presses toward is synonymous with the upward call of Jesus as the ultimate prize. *"Not that I have already obtained it or have already become perfect, but I press on so that I may lay hold of that for which also I was laid hold of by Christ Jesus. Brethren, I do not regard myself as having laid hold of it yet; but one thing I do: forgetting what lies behind and reaching forward to what lies ahead, I press on toward the goal for the prize of the upward call of God in Christ Jesus"* (Philippians 3:12-14).

After believers are raised bodily in the "first resurrection," the wicked will be resurrected at the Great White Throne Judgment one thousand years later and thrown into the lake of fire (Revelation 20:4-6; 11-15). This is why Jesus warned the church at Smyrna to be faithful until death so that they would receive the crown of life, which takes place at the Resurrection of the Righteous (Revelation 2:10b-11). The promises to the overcomer and the warnings against apostasy are vital today, when public sentiment is turning against Christians and the prophetic Scriptures are being fulfilled (Matthew 24:9-14; 2

Timothy 3:1-7; 12-13). When we read the great classic works on Christian martyrdom, like *Foxe's Book of Martyrs* and *Martyrs Mirror*, we see the warnings not to deny one's faith were in the mouths of those who persevered and were used by the Holy Spirit to preserve their souls from apostasy.

The book of Hebrews uses incredibly instructive words regarding finishing the race amidst the intense persecution they were suffering in the first century. When we read through the great "Hall of Faith" chapter in Hebrews 11, we discover: *"All these people were still living by faith when they died"* (Hebrews 11:13a). These saints finished their race and looked forward to the eternal, heavenly city not built with human hands (Hebrews 11:10).

After surveying this great cloud of witnesses who have gone before us, the author of Hebrews saves the best for last and encourages us to look to Jesus who, for the joy set before Him, endured the cross and sat down at the right hand of the Father: *"Therefore, since we have so great a cloud of witnesses surrounding us, let us also lay aside every encumbrance and the sin which so easily entangles us, and let us run with endurance the race that is set before us, fixing our eyes on Jesus, the author and perfecter of faith, who for the joy set before Him endured the cross, despising the shame, and has sat down at the right hand of the throne of God. For consider Him who has endured such hostility by sinners against Himself, so that you will not grow weary and lose heart"* (Hebrews 12:1-4).

Jesus taught, *"A disciple is not above his teacher, but everyone when he is fully trained will be like his teacher"* (Luke 6:40).

If we are Jesus' disciples, we must press on in the faith and finish the race set before us by looking to Jesus, who is *"the Apostle and High Priest of our confession"* (Hebrews 3:1). We need to fix "our eyes on Jesus, the author and perfecter of faith" (Hebrews 12:2). After encouraging believers to fix their eyes on Jesus who has gone before us and has finished His race triumphantly, the author of Hebrews then warns the children of God to accept God's discipline as a gracious Father who wants the best for His children. He informs us the Father is also our coach who is training us to finish the race so we may share in His holiness.

> *"For they disciplined us for a short time as seemed best to them, but he disciplines us for our good, so that we may share his holiness. All discipline for the moment seems not to be joyful, but sorrowful; yet to those who have been trained by it, afterwards it yields the peaceful fruit of righteousness"* (Hebrews 12:10-11).
>
> *"Pursue peace with all people, and holiness, without which no one will see the Lord"* (Hebrews 12:14).

The Apostle Paul also points Timothy to the Lord Jesus Christ as the prime example of running one's race to win. After the apostle Paul warns Timothy to fight the good fight of faith and lay hold of eternal life in his first letter, in his Second Epistle to Timothy, Paul rejoices because he has reached the finish line. He has fought the good fight, kept the faith, and finished his course, *"In pointing out these things to the brethren, you will be a good servant of Christ Jesus, constantly nourished on the words of the faith and of the sound doctrine which you have been following. But have nothing to do with worldly fables fit only for old women. On the other hand, discipline yourself for the purpose of godliness; for bodily discipline is only of little profit, but godliness is profitable for all things, since it holds promise for the present life and also for the life to come"* (2 Timothy 4:6-8). Paul is ready to face martyrdom with confidence because he has persevered to the end of the race and will receive the heavenly crown. It is important to note that the Crown of Righteousness and the Crown of Life are not special crowns rewarded to special believers. They are crowns that signify eternal life itself and are given to all believers.

How do we know this?

Paul states that the Crown of Righteousness will be given to "all who have loved His appearing" (2 Timothy 4:8). James declares the Crown of Life is "promised to those who love Him" (James 1:12). As Christians, we must confess Jesus Christ as Lord to be saved (Romans 10:9-10). According to the early church father, Tertullian, Nero executed the Apostle Paul because of his confession that Jesus Christ is Lord of all. In the same way, Timothy is to fight the good fight and hold on to his good confession that Jesus is Lord if he is to finish the race of faith.

I would like to close by leaving you with a few words of encouragement. So many professing Christians start the race of faith well but fail to finish because they rely on their own strength. We need to understand that as Christians, we cannot live the Christian life and finish the race of faith in our own power. We know we are saved by grace and not by our own good works (Ephesians 2:8-9), however most Christians are content to look back on saving grace but ignore that the Lord also wants to give us enabling and persevering grace. We are saved from our sins by Christ's death on the Cross through His saving grace, but we are strengthened to persevere by His enabling grace. The Lord desires for us to get past the finish line, but to do so, He must enable us to run our race through the power of the Holy Spirit. We must seek the Lord in prayer to empower and enable us with His Holy Spirit to finish the glorious race set before us.

> *"I bow my knees before the Father...*
>
> *...that He would grant you, according to the riches of His glory, to be strengthened with power through His Spirit in the inner man...*
>
> *...Now to Him who is able to do far more abundantly beyond all that we ask or think, according to the power that works within us"* (Ephesians 3:14, 16, 20).

Isaiah chapter 40, verse 31 says this: *"But to those who hope in the LORD will renew their strength. They will soar on wings like eagles; they will run and not grow weary, they will walk and not be faint."*

May each of us press on, wrestling with our faith to make our calling and election sure so that we may have an abundant entrance into Christ's eternal kingdom. And may each of us press on in the faith and pass the finish line, just as millions of faithful believers have done before us. May each of us hear these precious words of our Lord and Savior, Jesus Christ, on that final day: *"Well done, good and faithful servant. You have been faithful over a little; I will set you over much. Enter into the joy of your master"* (Matthew 25:23).

CHAPTER 12
DISCIPLING THROUGH THE SEVEN CHURCHES OF REVELATION

"Even the mysteries and difficulties of this book are united with discoveries of God, suited to impress the mind with awe, and purify the soul of the humble and attentive reader, though he may not discern the prophetic meaning."
– **Matthew Henry's Commentary**

HOW CAN I USE THE BOOK OF REVELATION TO DEMONSTRATE HOW WE SHOULD BE WRESTLING WITH DISCIPLESHIP?

I'VE ATTEMPTED to look at the examples of other teams and coaches and used them to compare or contrast my program with others. When it comes to coaching, there has always been much to learn from watching other teams and seeing how they perform practices, as well as how they coach in the corner and even after-the-match counseling. I've always believed in gleaning as much information as possible from as many sources as possible. There are coaches you want to imitate and copy, others who are more than a mixed bag, and others from whom you learn what *not* to do. This truth— found in raising up a young coach looking for guidance—is also found in the book of Revelation and among other verses of Scripture. But what many people don't recognize is that learning from the mistakes of others is a common theme in the Bible.

We can glean much by simply observing previous failures and not repeating them. In First Corinthians, chapter 10, verses 1-6, the Apostle Paul mentions some of these behaviors, which provides a valuable lesson for us:

> *"For I do not want you to be unaware, brethren, that our fathers were all under the cloud and all passed through the sea; and all were baptized into Moses in the cloud and in the sea; and all ate the same spiritual food; and all drank the same spiritual drink, for they were drinking from a spiritual rock which followed them; and the rock was Christ. Nevertheless, with most of them God was not well-pleased; for they were laid low in the wilderness. Now these things happened as examples for us, so that we would not crave evil things as they also craved."*

The mistakes Paul mentions of Israel here are included as a guardrail to keep us from falling in the same way. In fact, Paul says these very acts took place so that we would know not to crave evil things. This is to say there is still so much to learn while we are, at the same time, being warned about what had gone wrong in the past. With so much to be learned from the book of Revelation, I am saddened, and even frustrated, with the reluctance of so many teachers to bless those who listen to them to teach from this book. Especially when we consider that not reading, hearing, and heeding the words of the book means they are missing out on its promises. Revelation, chapter 1, verse 3 says, *"Blessed is the one who reads and those who hear the words of the prophecy, and heed the things which are written in it."*

This blessing is not only for those who lived when this was written but for all who hear its message. In fact, when it comes to the seven churches mentioned in the book of Revelation, the concluding statement to every church after the admonition, encouragement, or both, is the same:

"He who has an ear, let him hear what the Spirit says to the churches" (Revelation 2:7 – Ephesus).

"He who has an ear, let him hear what the Spirit says to the churches" (Revelation 2:11 – Smyrna).

"He who has an ear, let him hear what the Spirit says to the churches" (Revelation 2:17 – Pergamum).

"He who has an ear, let him hear what the Spirit says to the churches" (Revelation 2:29 – Thyatira).

"He who has an ear, let him hear what the Spirit says to the churches" (Revelation 3:6 – Sardis).

"He who has an ear, let him hear what the Spirit says to the churches" (Revelation 3:13 – Philadelphia).

"He who has an ear, let him hear what the Spirit says to the churches" (Revelation 3:22 – Laodicea).

Even if you are not well-versed in eschatology (the study of the end times), a walk among the seven golden lampstands is a blessing to discipleship. These seven churches encapsulate so much of what may occur in a church setting at any given moment. While our trust, rest, and fulfillment can only be found in Jesus, making sure the Church is in line with the Word of God is of great value as well. For the church is where we grow in our walk with Christ, and God willing, it is where your spouse and children will grow if you are blessed with raising them.

Looking at these churches, we can learn a lot about how we should walk with Christ and the pitfalls we must avoid. Of the seven churches, only two (Smyrna and Philadelphia) receive no rebuke from Christ. On the other hand, two churches receive a message containing admonition but are without commendation (Sardis and Laodicea). The other three churches (Ephesus, Pergamum, and Thyatira) all receive both a rebuke and an admonition. Considering that this message is meant to be heard by "whoever has an ear to hear what the Spirit says to the churches," we should look at these rebukes and admonitions and use them as guidelines for discipleship—how we are to act and how we are not to act.

Regarding the other churches, I have found them to encompass traits I love and characteristics I would not want to implement, such as the traits in Ephesus, Pergamum, or Thyatira. They had specific attributes in their church that Jesus commended, but they also had elements that should not be implemented or copied in any way, shape, or form. Then there were those akin to Smyrna and Philadelphia, where I would observe them and want to implement their style almost completely. There is much wisdom in a multitude of counselors, and learning from those who have gone before you is a tried-and-true recipe, which is the case with the churches in Revelation.

The lessons derived from the Seven Churches of Revelation are invaluable for our personal growth and the advancement of discipleship. Through studying these churches, we gain insights into maintaining a fervent love for Christ (as in Smyrna), standing firm in sound doctrine (as in Ephesus), and avoiding compromising love (as cautioned by the messages to Ephesus and Thyatira). Let us be diligent in applying these lessons to our lives, growing in Christ, and walking in the path of true discipleship. As we learn from the triumphs and failures of the seven churches, we are better equipped to navigate the challenges of discipleship, foster spiritual growth, and strengthen our relationship with God, as well as those we may someday serve. May the wisdom gleaned from these ancient churches inspire us to become more faithful, loving, and committed followers of Jesus Christ. Now let's take a look at what we can specifically learn from these churches.

When we look at the church in Ephesus, we find a church that does not put up with false doctrine. The church rebukes and roots it out immediately. Yet despite their solid doctrine, they have seemingly lost their first love. In attempting to do what is right, they have forgotten the reason why they are doing it! The church in Smyrna receives only a commendation. In fact, if we compare the churches of Smyrna and Philadelphia, both come from persecuted backgrounds, yet receive accolades. Both churches are also encouraged to continue in the faith, regardless of what is happening around them.

Smyrna was poor in the world's eyes, but God calls them rich, whereas the church of Laodicea had great wealth, but they were poor, blind, and naked. The church of Sardis had a reputation for being alive, but they were dead. God wanted Smyrna and Philadelphia to persevere and overcome, but He wanted repentance from Sardis and Laodicea. When considering our continual growth in Christ, we should be able to assess that we have not yet reached the level of Jesus. The Bible says we have been predestined to be conformed to the image of Jesus. But when we account for our lives and thoughts, we can quickly conclude none of us are there yet. When we equate the training of the body spiritually versus physically, both carry value, but the physical body is trumped by the spiritual one (1 Timothy 4:8). It's almost embarrassing to compare the two. But when we compare the two churches of Ephesus and

Thyatira, we see that both of them are having similar problems.

In his commentary on Revelation, Warren Wiersbe states, "Unloving orthodoxy and loving compromise are both hateful to God."[1] We do not want our adoration of a doctrine to become a wooden and unloving venture in sin-sniffing. Nor do we want our love for the lost to acquiesce, allowing sin to run rampant. So, how does this speak to us concerning discipleship?

It should lead us to have grace when those we disciple fall. We need to love them enough to bring them back into a healthy relationship with Jesus–the Way, the Truth, and the Life. Did God grant space for Jezebel, who was leading His servants astray, to repent? He certainly did! So, this means we also need to allow space for others to repent. But should we allow sin to run rampant in the church without it being restrained? Certainly not! The Bible clearly states that *"Faithful are the wounds of a friend, but deceitful are the kisses of an enemy"* (Proverbs 27:6).

Bringing the book of Revelation back to a regular part of our daily study will benefit our walk with Christ, as well as those to whom we are discipling. This isn't just an opinion on my part, it is affirmed with Scripture as previously cited.

> *"Blessed is the one who reads and those who hear the words of the prophecy and heeds the things which are written in it"* – Revelation 1:3.

CHAPTER 13
EMBRACE THE GRIND

"How many, even young, healthy men, are too lazy either to walk or ride! They waste away in gentle activity [...] luxury increases sloth, unfitting for excessive either of body or mind..."
– **John Wesley**

WHILE GROWING UP, sports was a prerequisite in my family. Watching the Dodgers, Lakers, and Cowboys games as a family was something we always did together, and I loved watching them. At the time, the only aspect of my life that was better than watching a Dodgers game with the family was playing sports while my family cheered me on. I played baseball, football, and basketball – each was enjoyable and demanded dedication. That being said, none compared to the unparalleled challenges I would face when I joined the sport of wrestling. Looking back, I realize that if I hadn't known what to expect when I entered wrestling, I might not have known the toughness it would take to persevere through the daunting training required to compete in the sport.

When it came to baseball, I found my passion as a catcher. The thrill of catching pitches, perfecting my technique in blocking the plate, and throwing out runners trying to steal a base ignited my love for the sport. Batting, of course, was an exhilarating aspect that never failed to bring joy to my heart. Basketball, on the other hand, provided a different kind of excitement. Though there were sprints to run, the simplistic pleasure of shooting a basketball is one in which even the most inexperienced practitioner can find enjoyment. As for football, the rigorous practices were tough, but the satisfaction of hitting opponents on the field was immensely gratifying for any young guy. While football probably prepared me most for what would be happening to me physically and mentally, it didn't even approach what I found in wrestling. During my first practice, I knew wrestling stood far apart from the other sports.

The fragrant aroma of bleach, high school boys' body odor, and a stale knee pad someone didn't wash after using for half a season is the mixture of scents few forget, though most wrestlers grow accustomed to them after only a few days of practice. That first time breaking through a limit of exhaustion you didn't even know you had is embedded in our minds but paid dividends later in life. As the great Dan Gable said, "Once you've wrestled, everything else in life is easy." That's because of the intense nature of the training. As many football players who joined wrestling after their season was finished learned the hard way, what they called "hell week," wrestlers simply called "a Tuesday." Unfortunately, this is why so many of my friends I convinced to join left the sport before truly comprehending it.

I had one advantage many of my friends who ended up quitting didn't have—a solid warning from my brothers about what it would take, and what I should expect when I stepped into the gym. They painted a realistic picture of what I would face, cautioning me about the physical and mental demands that would be placed upon me. They spoke of the many who would quit in the first week, unable to handle the intensity. Their counsel gave me insight into what would be required of me, and it served as a driving force that enabled me to face the grueling challenges head-on. Although the allure of pursuing other sports for a more carefree experience was tempting, wrestling held a special place in my heart. And the struggles and sacrifices I endured on the wrestling mat taught me the value of discipline, dedication, and perseverance.

If there was one statement that encapsulates the life of a wrestler—which has been declared a maxim for wrestlers and their coaches—it is none other than "embrace the grind." This motto typifies the grit and grind it takes to become an elite wrestler and the work that needs to be embraced. Over the door of my wrestling room, a sign reads, "If you are not bleeding or sweating, something is wrong." But for most wrestlers who have travailed through any length of a season, the statement, "If you are not bleeding *and* sweating, something is wrong," would better fit the bill. The wrestler immediately learns that the work output during a six-minute match is infinitesimal compared to the practice week. And if you don't embrace the difficult, you'll never come close to achieving the glory.

The agonizing training would only make sense to the wrestler, as the small amount of glory (extremely small) and a tiny amount of hardware will never fulfill what is found in the glory of the agony.

Motivational videos are common in this day and age. Not all of them, however, include one of the most decorated wrestlers of all time - a voice you hear that gives the impetus for the adversity you will face and the motivation to face it. In one particular "Cage Fighter" brand campaign, Jordan Burroughs, a six-time world champion wrestler, says the following:

> *"The Grind. It's what separates me from my opponent. It's what lets me know I'm doing what it takes to win. The Grind beats you up. It wears you down. It knocks you to the ground and whispers in your ear, 'Is that all you got?' The Grind picks you up. It pulls you forward. And when the time comes to reach down through the pain and weakness for that last little bit of strength you've got left, The Grind's got your back. The Grind can't be tamed. It can't be compromised. It can't be put off till tomorrow cuz you don't feel like it today. The Grind pushes you through defeat. The Grind lifts you up in victory. I don't fear The Grind, I respect it. I don't avoid The Grind, I Embrace it."*
> 1

Who is Jordan Burroughs? Well, let's take a look and see

why he is qualified to motivate others to "Embrace the Grind." Here is a list of some of his freestyle wrestling accomplishments:

2011 Pan American Games Champion - 74 kg
2011 US Open Champion - 74 kg
2011 World Champion - 74 kg
2012 US Open Champion - 74 kg
2012 World Cup Champion - 74 kg
2012 Olympic Champion - 74 kg
2013 World Cup Champion - 74 kg
2013 US Open Champion - 74kg
2013 World Champion - 74kg
2014 US Open Champion - 74kg
2014 World Championships Bronze Medal Winner - 74kg
2015 World Cup Champion - 74 kg
2015 Pan American Games Champion - 74kg
2015 World Champion - 74kg
2016 Olympian - 74kg
2017 U.S. Open Champion - 74 kg
2017 World Cup Champion - 74 kg
2017 World Champion - 74kg
2018 World Bronze Medalist - 74kg
2019 Pan American Games Champion - 74kg
2019 World Bronze Medalist - 74kg
2021 World Champion -79Kg
2022 World Champion 79Kg

Jordan Burroughs is one of the most decorated wrestlers of

all time. If there is anyone who knows how to "Embrace the Grind," it's Jordan Burroughs. The Grind has been embraced by world champions all around the world and in every sport. The Grind's philosophy works for every great business venture and for every Christian ministry. Not only has Burroughs embraced "The Grind," he has also embraced Jesus.

According to his personal testimony, he originally came to Christ at seventeen but admittedly gave in to the many temptations that college had to offer before fully dedicating his life to Jesus on December 19, 2009. In his testimony, he warned about his own idolatry from which he needed to repent. Regarding what it takes to win a gold medal and how Christians must strive to enter the narrow gate, he referenced Matthew 7:13.[2]

A benefit we receive from testimonies like Jordan's is that they remind us of the dangers and temptations that could come our way. Testimonies can show us our need for the Savior, regardless of whether we have reached the pinnacle of our sport or our life. These warnings greatly help discipleship and should show us where the Devil might try to draw us away from the straight and narrow. This is also a chief task in discipleship as we prepare new Christians to know precisely what they're signing up for! After a number of people began to follow Him, Jesus gave the people a hard message to chew on. He wanted them to understand and count the cost of what it would take to follow Him.

> "Now large crowds were going along with Him; and He turned and said to them, 'If anyone comes to Me, and does not hate his

own father and mother and wife and children and brothers and sisters, yes, and even his own life, he cannot be My disciple. Whoever does not carry his own cross and come after Me cannot be My disciple. For which one of you, when he wants to build a tower, does not first sit down and calculate the cost to see if he has enough to complete it? Otherwise, when he has laid a foundation and is not able to finish, all who observe it begin to ridicule him, saying, 'This man began to build and was not able to finish'" (Luke 14:25-30).

There are a number of lessons to be learned here. One is to understand the historical context in which it was written. In our modern times, when we think about "picking up our cross," it is typically viewed through a romanticized understanding that makes us think of a necklace or trendy tattoo. But when Jesus said this, He was calling people to take upon themselves a symbol of shameful execution. The cross could be similar to someone today requiring us to pick up our electric chair or noose as a symbol of dying daily and sacrificing our lives in this world for discipleship in Christ.

To emphasize this point to an even greater extent, He not only calls us to "execute" our own desires each day, but He also says we have to count the cost first to be sure that we can endure. Here, we find Jesus calling His disciples to make sure they do what is described over and over again in the final book of the New Testament—endure and persevere. But not only that, He wants to make sure believers are able to do that before agreeing to be discipled by the King of Kings. Jesus wants to ensure that the worries and affairs of this world, the deceitfulness of riches, persecution, and the Devil will not get in the way after a disciple has made the commitment to follow Him. Embracing the Grind, so to speak, is about picking up our cross and following Jesus each day. In fact, Jesus used a Greek word to describe the agonizing training athletes in His day would go through in order to win a perishable crown.

The Greek word "ἀγωνίζομαι" (agonizimai) is used to describe entering through the "narrow door" by Jesus Himself: *"Strive to enter through the narrow door; for many, I tell you, will seek to enter and will not be able"* (Luke 13:24).

The root of agonizimai (agōn) is used in several other word variations to convey the meaning of being a combatant in public games, to contend, fight, labor, or strive earnestly. The Apostle Paul used a word with the root (agōn) to describe his labor for the Kingdom. *"We proclaim Him, admonishing every man and teaching every man with all wisdom, so that we may present every man complete in Christ. For this purpose also I labor, striving (ἀγωνιζόμενος) according to His power, which mightily works within me"* – Colossians 1:28-29

The labor of Epaphras is mentioned as well. Colossians, chapter 4, verse 12 says: *"Epaphras, who is one of your number, a bondslave of Jesus Christ, sends you his greetings, always laboring (ἀγωνιζόμενος) earnestly for you in his prayers, that you may stand perfect and fully assured in all the will of God."*

Another word is also used with the same root (agōn) to describe the "bout" that we are supposed to take up in the good fight of faith. *"Fight (ἀγωνίζου) the good fight of faith; take hold of the eternal life to which you were called, and you made the good confession in the presence of many witnesses"* (1 Timothy 6:12). And in Second Timothy, chapter 4, verse 7, we read: *"I have fought* (ἠγώνισμαι) *the good fight, I have finished the course, I have kept the faith."*

But for the purpose of the Grind, Paul mentions the amount of self-control it takes to be a man of competition, specifically for runners, though, no doubt wrestlers could apply this as well. *"Everyone who competes* (ἀγωνιζόμενος) *in the games exercises self-control in all things. They then do it to receive a perishable wreath, but we an imperishable"* (1 Corinthians 9:25).

The immediate context in this verse expresses an important truth regarding believers and their self-control.

> *"Do you not know that those who run in a race all run, but only one receives the prize? Run in such a way that you may win. Everyone who competes in the games, exercises self-control in all things. They then do it to receive a perishable wreath, but we an imperishable. Therefore, I run in such a way, as not without aim; I box in such a way, as not beating the air; but I discipline my body and make it my slave, so that, after I have preached to others, I myself will not be disqualified"* (1 Corinthians 9:24-27).

As you can see, Paul was able to use sports frequently as an analogy that people could easily understand. He knew that those in Corinth would know what it took to compete at a high level and called believers to "embrace the grind" in a way that competes for a crown that will never perish!

The author of Hebrews also exhorts us and reminds us of the issues that hinder our performance. While partying, drinking, and unbiblical relationships obviously impede our walk with Christ, there are other things that burden us on a regular basis. In Hebrews, we are admonished to lay aside the sin and the "excess weight" that holds us down, keeping us from running our race.

> *"Therefore, since we have so great a cloud of witnesses surrounding us, let us also lay aside every encumbrance and the sin which so easily entangles us, and let us run with endurance the race that is set before us, fixing our eyes on Jesus, the author and perfecter of faith, who for the joy set before Him endured the cross, despising the shame, and has sat down at the right hand of the throne of God."* (Hebrews 12:1-2).

The "encumbrance" spoken about is any extra "thing" that might hold a person down and impede their run. We are to shed this extra weight so we can run our race with endurance! This is "The Grind" we must embrace every day. We must lay aside anything that is hindering us from fully seeking Christ and embracing "The Grind" just as Christ embraced it for you!

CHAPTER 14
OUR LAST MATCH

"It is grace at the beginning, and grace at the end. So that when you and I come to lie upon our death beds, the one thing that should comfort and help and strengthen us there is the thing that helped us in the beginning. Not what we have been, not what we have done, but the Grace of God in Jesus Christ our Lord. The Christian life starts with grace, it must continue with grace, it ends with grace. Grace wondrous grace. By the grace of God, I am what I am. Yet not I, but the Grace of God which was with me."
– **Martyn Lloyd-Jones**

BECAUSE OF THE nature of the postseason, unless a wrestler enters into the "placing rounds" of the final tournament, they don't know when their last match will take place. It can be quite a treacherous walk off the mat, as all of the blood, sweat, and tears come to an abrupt end at the sound of the final whistle blow. I still remember my last match like it was yesterday.

After needing to default because of an injury in the semi-finals of our CIF tournament, I thought I could limp my way into the next portion of the qualifying tournament by winning a couple of matches in the morning and then defaulting after I had qualified. I have never been one to give up a lot of points in a match, but I gave up a five-point move to start the one-minute consolation round and found myself playing catch up for the next two rounds. I had to pick the top position because of the deficit in the third round, and I finished the match, turning my opponent multiple times, but I was not able to get the fall I needed to secure the win. It was one of those matches where I felt if I wrestled it one hundred times, I would have come out the victor ninety-nine of those times. But speculations and excuses mean nothing in this sport, and I can still remember walking off the mat alone, devastated by the premature end of my career as a high school wrestler.

I sat alone in the hot sun with the black asphalt of a parking lot swallowing up my tears as they rained down my face, representing my own failed expectations. I was encouraged when I was told that college wrestling was what matters and that's where my focus needed to go. But I didn't want my name displayed on my high school's wall as the team captain of the "shoulda, woulda, couldas," and no amount of college accolades was going to fix that.

While this cold reality came true for me and my own

personal accolades, I have dedicated my life to coaching the sport of wrestling, and I've been able to warn people of the key mistakes that led me down this path. I've been blessed to help erase names that could have ended up on the "Wall of Failed Expectations," and I have seen many wrestlers reach goals they never thought possible. Just as I was not a Christian for the first part of my life, I know the pitfalls and places where people fall. I can see the dangers from a mile away and help others avoid the same dreadful pits. While I never got to achieve the goals I'd hoped to reach in my youth, I realized that in Christ, my goal has completely shifted. My mind has been renewed and I know when it comes to wrestling, or anything else the Lord puts before me, there is nothing done in vain when it is done by and through the Lord. For those in Christ, if you are doing your work for Christ, it is never in vain. Whether people to whom we minister come to Christ or not, we aren't doing these works to put more notches on our belts.

"Therefore, my beloved brethren, be steadfast, immovable, always abounding in the work of the Lord, knowing that your toil is not in vain in the Lord" (1 Corinthians 15:58).

"Therefore" in the above text is connected to the previous chapter in which Paul explains our confidence in the afterlife, which is based upon the confidence in the public resurrection of Jesus before over five hundred witnesses (1 Corinthians 15:1-4). It speaks to the fact that death has now been rendered into the loser's bracket where it will eventually be knocked out of the tournament eternally.

> *"But when this perishable body puts on the imperishable, and this mortal body puts on immortality, then will come about the saying that is written, 'Death is swallowed up in victory. O death, where is your victory? O death, where is your sting?' The sting of death is sin, and the power of sin is the law; but thanks be to God, who gives us the victory through our Lord Jesus Christ"* (1 Corinthians 15:54-57).

This is what the "therefore" in verse 58 is there for—to connect the end result of victory in Christ with our labor of today. While we "embrace the grind" and do our work for the Lord, we know that none of our labor—accomplished in and for the Lord—is for nothing. There is also an importance for believers to understand our own mortality and to recognize that we have one shot to know Christ and one shot to help others know Him!

Moses prayed: *"So, teach us to number our days, that we may present to you a heart of wisdom"* (Psalm 90:12). And it is wise to recognize that we can forget to number our days, so we should ask God to teach us to remember this. James wrote not to list what you are going to do without consulting the Lord, for *"... you do not know what your life will be like tomorrow. You are just a vapor that appears for a little while and then vanishes away"* (James 4:14).

These scriptures have helped me understand that life is a

vapor, and we only have one shot at using our gifts and talents to make an impact for Christ. I wasted so many years of my life running after things that will not matter in eternity, but I'm determined not to waste any more of them.

I'd like to share a poem that helped shape my walk with Christ when I first heard it as a younger believer. Sometimes, I would be consumed with the reality of my own personal sin and struggled to fathom why God would forgive me. Even after I travailed through the enemy's attack on my own personal salvation, the thing I kept thinking about was the time I wasted. But the Lord opened my eyes to the reality of the time we have before us and the impact we can have today if we don't allow ourselves to succumb to the enemy, who tries to drag us into "paralysis by analysis." We must not allow him to hinder us from running a good race and producing fruit for the kingdom. This poem was written by a real stud! C.T. Studd, to be exact, and its stanzas will forever be embedded in my heart.

C.T. was a missionary to the Congo, China, and other regions, but he was also a famous cricket player before his conversion. His most famous poem is the one that changed my walk as a young believer, and I'd just bet it can change your walk as well. I am ending this book with this poem because I'm calling you to discipleship, believers. Be someone's spiritual wrestling partner in their walk with Christ and do so recognizing that we only have one life to live. So use it for what will ultimately matter most!

"Only One Life, 'Twill Soon Be Past"
By C.T. Studd

Two little lines I heard one day,
Traveling along life's busy way;
Bringing conviction to my heart,
And from my mind would not depart;
Only one life, 'twill soon be past,
Only what's done for Christ will last.

Only one life, yes only one,
Soon will its fleeting hours be done;
Then, in 'that day' my Lord to meet,
And stand before His Judgement seat;
Only one life, 'twill soon be past,
Only what's done for Christ will last.

Only one life, the still small voice,
Gently pleads for a better choice
Bidding me selfish aims to leave,
And to God's holy will to cleave;
Only one life, 'twill soon be past,
Only what's done for Christ will last.

Only one life, a few brief years,
Each with its burdens, hopes, and fears;
Each with its clays I must fulfill.
living for self or in His will;

Only one life, 'twill soon be past,
Only what's done for Christ will last.

When this bright world would tempt me sore,
When Satan would a victory score;
When self would seek to have its way,
Then help me Lord with joy to say;
Only one life, 'twill soon be past,
Only what's done for Christ will last.

Give me Father, a purpose deep,
In joy or sorrow Thy word to keep;
Faithful and true what e'er the strife,
Pleasing Thee in my daily life;
Only one life, 'twill soon be past,,
Only what's done for Christ will last.

Oh let my love with fervor burn,
And from the world now let me turn;
Living for Thee, and Thee alone,
Bringing Thee pleasure on Thy throne;
Only one life, 'twill soon be past,
Only what's done for Christ will last.
Only one life, yes only one,

Now let me say, "Thy will be done";
And when at last I'll hear the call,
I know I'll say "twas worth it all";

Only one life, "twill soon be past,
Only what's done for Christ will last."

__Extra stanza__
Only one life, 'twill soon be past,
Only what's done for Christ will last.
And when I am dying, how happy I'll be,
If the lamp of my life has been burned out for Thee."

NOTES

INTRODUCTION

1. Mark Munoz, "UFC Contender Mark Munoz Talks Faith, Family and Being Drug-Free" by John Crandall, Patch.com, October 25, 2011

CHAPTER 2

1. A.W. Tozer, *Discipleship: What it Truly Means to be a Christian*, pg. 1.
2. Marvin Richardson Vincent, *Word Studies in the New Testament, Vol. I*, New York: Charles Scribner's Sons, 1887
3. Martina Gracin, Discipleship in the Context of Judaism in Jesus' Time, Part 1, pg. 212.
4. Ibid., pg. 212-213.
5. Ibid., pg. 217.

CHAPTER 4

1. Irenaeus, *Against Heresies*, Book 1, Chapter 10
2. Catechetical Lecture 5.12, St. Cyril of Jerusalem.
3. The Epistle of Mathetes to Diognetus, Chapter 5, The Manners of the Christians.
4. Ibid., Chapter 6, The Relation of Christians to the World.

CHAPTER 5

1. Henry D.M Spence, *The Complete Pulpit Commentary*, Volume 7, Matthew to John.
2. *The Cambridge Bible for Schools and Colleges*, Volume 37, pg. 173.
3. Barnes' Notes on 2 Timothy 3.

4. Clarke's Commentary on Psalm 1.
5. J. Vernon McGee, *Thru the Bible*, pg. 847.

CHAPTER 6

1. Tremper Longman, *The Fear of the Lord is Wisdom*, pg. 10.
2. Tremper Longman, *The Fear of the Lord is Wisdom*, pg. 13.
3. Derek Kidner, *Proverbs*, pg. 31
4. Ibid.
5. Clement of Rome, *First Epistle to the Corinthians*, Chapter 21:6.
6. Dr. John Oswalt, "Should We Unhitch from the Old Testament with Dr. John Oswalt," Good Fight Ministries YouTube channel, Nov. 8, 2021.
7. Alexander Maclaren, *Expositions of the Holy Scripture*: "Love and Fear: 1 John 4:18," pg. 358.

CHAPTER 7

1. A.W. Tozer, *Discipleship: What it Truly Means to be a Christian–Collected Insights from A.W. Tozer*, pg. 8.

CHAPTER 8

1. Charles Haddon Spurgeon, "*She Was Not Hid*," 1888 Sermon at the Metropolitan Tabernacle.
2. *Martyrdom of Saint Polycarp*, Bishop of Smyrna, Letter of the Church of Smyrna to the Church of Pilomelium, Chapter 1.
3. Charles Haddon Spurgeon, "The Wailing of Risca," Sermon No. 349, December 9th, 1860: Exeter Hall, Strand.
4. Leonard Ravenhill, *Why Revival Tarries*, pg. 32.

CHAPTER 9

1. S. Cyril of Jerusalem, *Nicene and Post-Nicene Fathers*, Second Series, Vol. 7, Five Catechetical Lectures: Lecture 19, pg.146

CHAPTER 11

1. A. T. Robertson, *Word Pictures In the New Testament*, Vol. IV, pg. 150.

CHAPTER 12

1. Warren Wiersbe, *The Bible Exposition Commentary: New Testament, Volume 2*, Ephesians – Revelation, pg. 575.

CHAPTER 13

1. Jordan Burroughs, "The Grind," CFATHLETIC YouTube Channel, 2012.
2. Jordan Burrough's Testimony, Lighthouse Ministries: YouTube Channel, 2016.

ACKNOWLEDGMENTS

I extend my deepest gratitude to the dedicated editing team whose unwavering commitment elevated every facet of this book. Special thanks to Ted Hollis and Melissa Service for their meticulous editing contributions that enhanced the overall quality of the book.

I am indebted to Doug Stebleton, whose role extended beyond editing and proofreading to encompass project leadership, steering it toward successful completion. His guidance and dedication have been invaluable.

A heartfelt acknowledgment goes to Tony Palacio, not only an adept editor but also the creative genius behind the captivating cover art that visually represents the essence of the book.

Lastly, I extend my sincere appreciation to my pastor and father-in-law, Joe Schimmel, whose profound influence not only inspired the creation of this book, but also played a pivotal role in shaping my ability to express these thoughts. His guidance and mentorship have been instrumental throughout this writing journey, and I'm so blessed that he also contributed an entire chapter to the book!

ABOUT THE AUTHOR

Chad Davidson is an elder and youth ministry pastor at Blessed Hope Chapel in Simi Valley, CA.

He is also an integral part of Good Fight Ministries, an apologetics and discernment ministry discussing contemporary issues in pop culture in light of the Bible. Chad is the host of two popular podcast shows, The Good Fight Radio Show and 5:11 News with Chad Davidson. Both shows broadcast on all major podcast platforms, and on the official Good Fight Ministries YouTube channel. Chad has also been a wrestling coach since 2008.

Chad, his wife Holly, and their four children are actively involved in street evangelism and international ministries, which include ongoing mission trips to Central America, Europe, and the Middle East, reflecting the love of Christ and God's redemptive message of hope.

If you enjoyed this book, please take a moment to write a brief review on Amazon and/or Goodreads. We appreciate and look forward to reading your comments about Wrestling With Discipleship.

To learn more about Chad or Wrestling with Discipleship, please visit: <u>wrestlingwithdiscipleship.com.</u>

Thank you and God bless!

www.ingramcontent.com/pod-product-compliance
Lightning Source LLC
Chambersburg PA
CBHW070152100426
42743CB00013B/2883